The New Waffle Cookbook

A Waffle Maker Cookbook with Delicious Waffle Recipes

By
BookSumo Press
All rights reserved

Published by
http://www.booksumo.com

ENJOY THE RECIPES?

KEEP ON COOKING
WITH 6 MORE FREE COOKBOOKS!

Visit our website and simply enter your email address to join the club and receive your 6 cookbooks.

http://booksumo.com/magnet

https://www.instagram.com/booksumopress/

https://www.facebook.com/booksumo/

LEGAL NOTES

All Rights Reserved. No Part Of This Book May Be Reproduced Or Transmitted In Any Form Or By Any Means. Photocopying, Posting Online, And / Or Digital Copying Is Strictly Prohibited Unless Written Permission Is Granted By The Book's Publishing Company. Limited Use Of The Book's Text Is Permitted For Use In Reviews Written For The Public.

Table of Contents

Manitoba Molasses Waffles 9

How to Make Waffle Batter 10

Belgian Wheat Waffles 11

Brown Rice Potato Waffles 12

Spice Mid-Autumn Waffles 13

West Virginia French Toast Waffles 14

Kentucky Blueberry Waffles 15

Spiced Cardamom Waffl 16

Sourdough Waffles 17

Pecan Honey Oat Waffles 18

Moonlight Waffles 19

Buttermilk Gingerbread Waffles 20

Kindergarten Lunch Box Waffles 21

Carol's Cornmeal Waffles 22

State Fair Waffles 23

3-Grains Oatmeal Waffles 24

Mexican Hash Brown Waffles 25

Houston Waffles 26

Cinnamon Pinwheel Waffles 27

Belgian Waffles 101 28

Madison Oat Waffles 29

Enhanced Toasted Waffles 30

Ice Cream Waffle Sandwiches 31

Country Cottage Waffles 32

Banana Waffles with Extras 33

Sweetened Flax Waffles 35

Victorian Waffles 36

Yam Waffles 37

Twin City Waffles 38

Light Oat Waffles 39

Vegan Almond Waffles 40

Crispy Waffles 101 41

How to Make a Liege Waffle 42

July's Zesty Waffles 43

Apple, Walnuts, and Pumpkin Waffles 44

Florida Duplex Waffles with Vanilla Syrup 45

Waffles Stockholm 46

Gingery Pumpkin Waffles 47

Willie Mae's Buttermilk Waffles 48

Rochester Lemon Waffles 49

Spelman Seltzer Waffles 50

London Butterscotch Waffles 51

Waffles Augusta Autumn 52

Corn on Oats Waffles 53

Coffee Bisquick Waffles 54

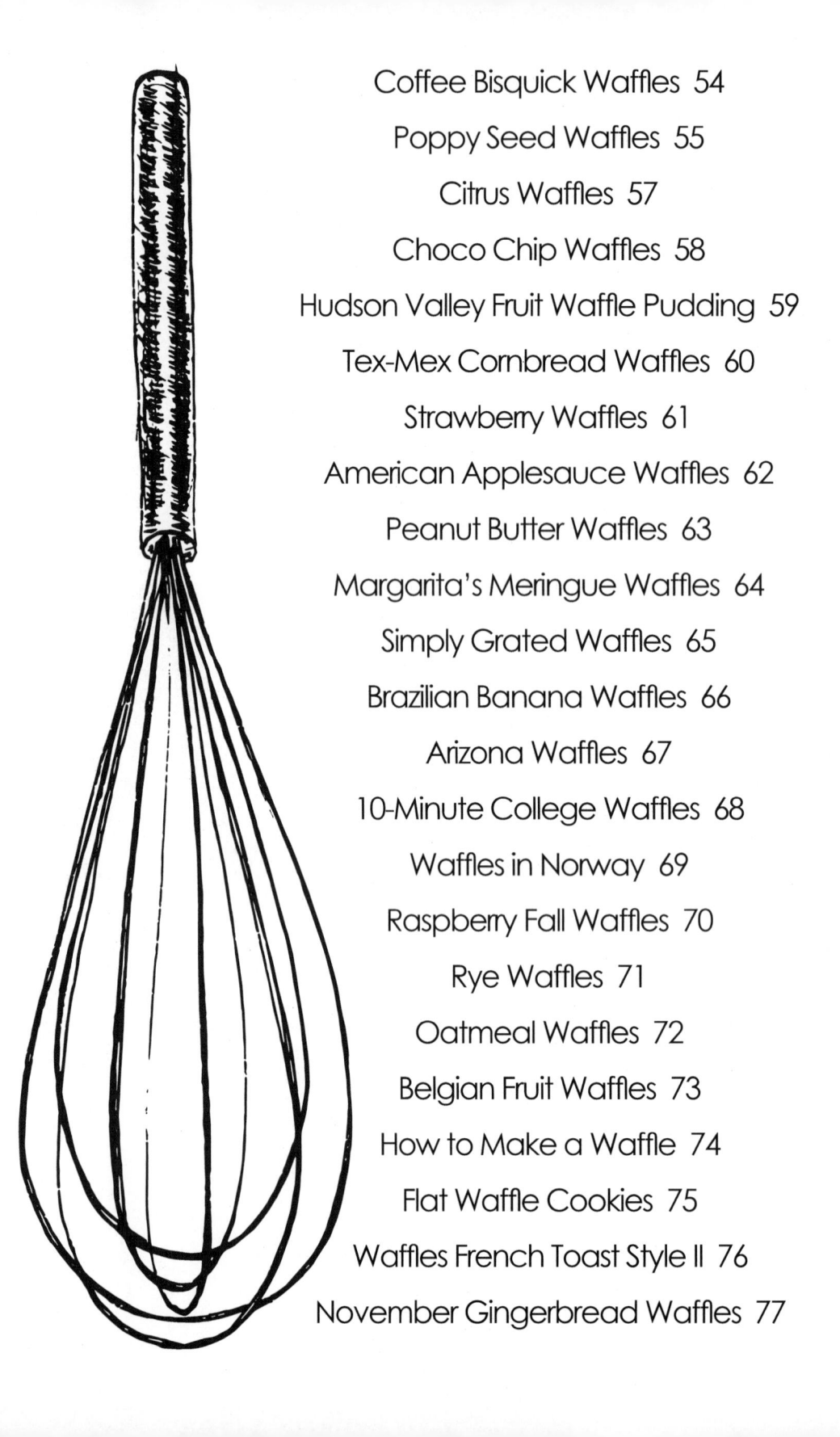

Poppy Seed Waffles 55

Citrus Waffles 57

Choco Chip Waffles 58

Hudson Valley Fruit Waffle Pudding 59

Tex-Mex Cornbread Waffles 60

Strawberry Waffles 61

American Applesauce Waffles 62

Peanut Butter Waffles 63

Margarita's Meringue Waffles 64

Simply Grated Waffles 65

Brazilian Banana Waffles 66

Arizona Waffles 67

10-Minute College Waffles 68

Waffles in Norway 69

Raspberry Fall Waffles 70

Rye Waffles 71

Oatmeal Waffles 72

Belgian Fruit Waffles 73

How to Make a Waffle 74

Flat Waffle Cookies 75

Waffles French Toast Style II 76

November Gingerbread Waffles 77

Cinnamon Ginger Waffles 78

Skytop Waffles 79

PB&J Waffles 80

Maryland Chicken Waffles 81

Cake Flour Waffles 83

Simple Vanilla Waffles 84

Georgia Peach and Biscuit Waffles 85

Dijon Buttermilk Waffles 87

Waffle Sandwiches 88

Country Crispy Waffles 89

Green Feta Waffles 90

Leftover Rice Waffles with Spiced Syrup 91

Lunch Pizza Waffles 92

4-Ingredient American Breakfast 93

Sweet Mediterranean Waffles 94

Cornmeal Cereal Waffles 95

Honey Hazel Waffles 96

Vegetarian Soy Waffles 97

Rachela's Red Velvet Waffles 98

Canadian Chocolate Waffles 99

Cute Waffles 100

Vegan Papaya and Orange Waffles 101

Spicy Cheddar Waffles 102

Seattle Waffles with Avocados 103

Full Georgia Breakfast 104

Waffles Brulee 105

Saratoga Flax Waffles 106

Yuan's Chinese Egg Waffles 107

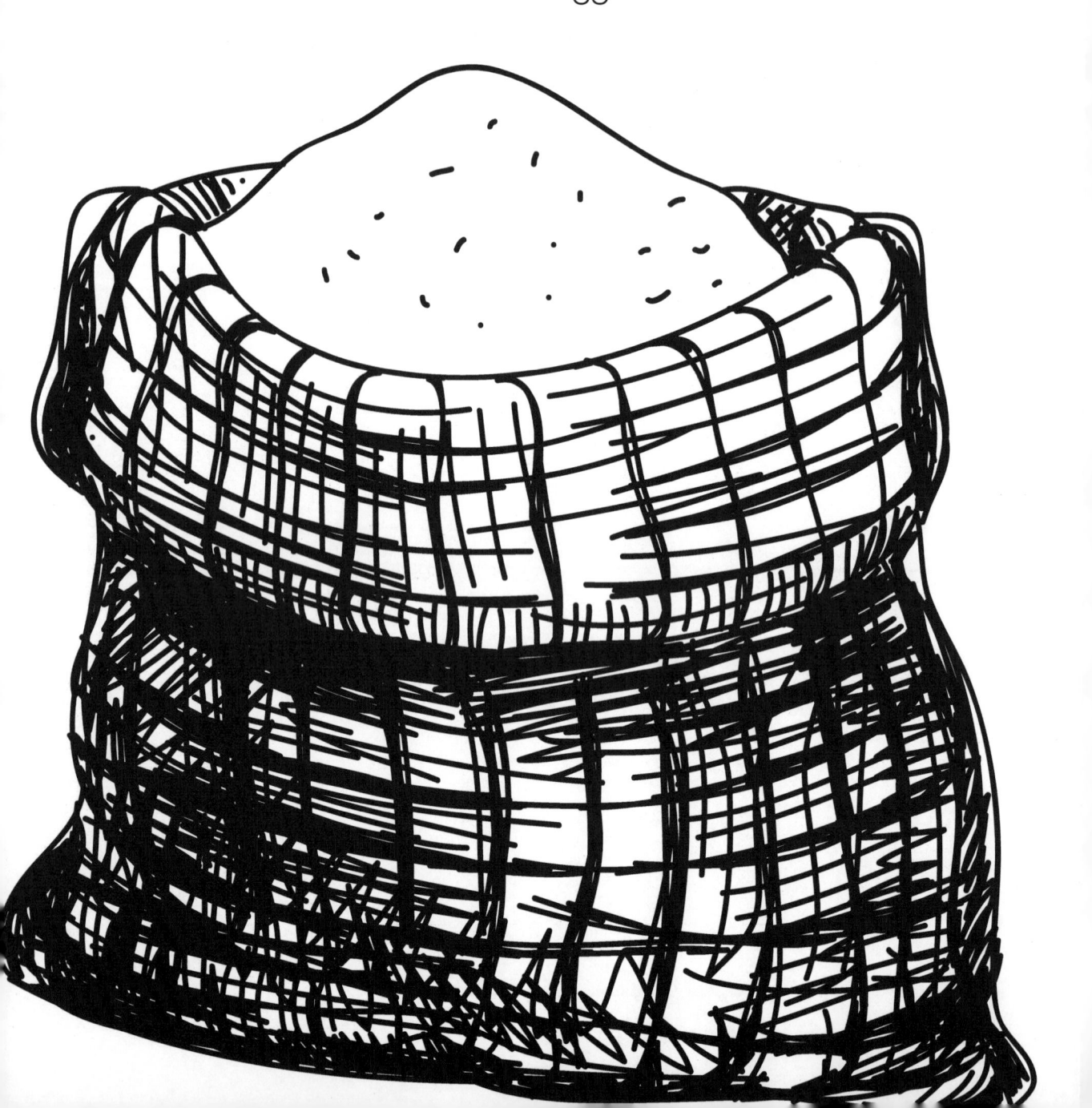

Manitoba Molasses Waffles

Prep Time: 4 mins
Total Time: 10 mins

Servings per Recipe: 1
Calories   105.7
Fat   2.4g
Cholesterol   18.6mg
Sodium   351.4mg
Carbohydrates   17.6g
Protein   3.4g

Ingredients

2 C. quick oats
1/2 C. flour
1 tsp salt
1 1/2 C. water
1 tbsp baking powder

1 beaten egg
1 tbsp molasses
2 tbsp corn oil

Directions

1. Set your waffle iron and lightly, grease it.
2. In a bowl, add all ingredients and mix until well combined.
3. Add desired amount of the mixture in waffle iron and cook as suggested by the manufacturer.
4. Repeat with the remaining mixture.
5. Enjoy warm.

HOW TO
Waffle Batter

Prep Time: 10 mins
Total Time: 20 mins

Servings per Recipe: 6
Calories	345.2
Fat	16.5g
Cholesterol	71.4mg
Sodium	433.1mg
Carbohydrates	39.9g
Protein	8.6g

Ingredients

2 eggs
1 2/3 C. milk
1/3 C. vegetable oil
2 C. all-purpose flour
1 tbsp baking powder

2 tbsp sugar
1/2 tsp salt
1 tsp vanilla
1 tsp maple extract

Directions

1. Set your waffle iron and lightly, grease it.
2. In a bowl, mix together the flour, sugar, baking powder and salt.
3. In another bowl, add remaining ingredients and beat until well combined.
4. Add flour mixture and mix until just combined.
5. Add desired amount of the mixture in waffle iron and cook as suggested by the manufacturer.
6. Repeat with the remaining mixture.
7. Enjoy warm.

Belgian Wheat Waffles

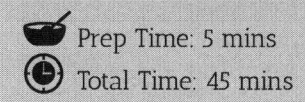

Prep Time: 5 mins
Total Time: 45 mins

Servings per Recipe: 16
Calories   137.3
Fat   6.9g
Cholesterol   39.1mg
Sodium   205.7mg
Carbohydrates   15.6g
Protein   4.1g

Ingredients

- 2 C. whole wheat flour
- 1/4 C. sugar
- 3 tsp baking powder
- 3/4 tsp salt
- 2 C. milk
- 3 eggs
- 1/3 C. vegetable oil
- 1 tsp vanilla extract

Directions

1. Set your waffle iron and lightly, grease it.
2. In a bowl, add the flour, baking powder, sugar and salt and mix well.
3. Add the eggs, oil, and milk and stir until blended.
4. Add about 1/3 C. of the mixture into the waffle iron and cook as suggested by the manufacturer.
5. Repeat with the remaining mixture.
6. Enjoy warm.

BROWN RICE
Potato Waffles

Prep Time: 8 mins
Total Time: 23 mins

Servings per Recipe: 1
Calories	352.5
Fat	14.5g
Cholesterol	77.3mg
Sodium	727.3mg
Carbohydrates	46.8g
Protein	8.9g

Ingredients

1 C. brown rice flour
1/2 C. potato starch
1/4 C. tapioca flour
2 tsp baking powder
1 tsp salt

1/4 C. oil
2 eggs
1 1/2 C. buttermilk
1 tsp sugar

Directions

1. In a bowl, add all the ingredients and mix until well combined.
2. Add desired amount of the mixture in waffle iron and cook as suggested by the manufacturer.
3. Repeat with the remaining mixture.
4. Enjoy warm.

Spice Mid-Autumn Waffles

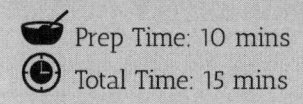

Prep Time: 10 mins
Total Time: 15 mins

Servings per Recipe: 1
Calories   227.1
Fat   9.2g
Cholesterol   68.8mg
Sodium   403.8mg
Carbohydrates   30.5g
Protein   6.1g

Ingredients

- 1 1/2 C. all-purpose flour
- 3 tsp baking powder
- 1/2 tsp baking soda
- 1 tsp cinnamon
- 1 tsp nutmeg
- 1 tsp ground ginger
- 1 pinch salt
- 2 eggs
- 1/4 C. packed brown sugar
- 1 C. canned pumpkin puree
- 1 2/3 C. milk
- 4 tbsp butter, melted and cooled

Directions

1. In a bowl, add the flour, baking soda, baking powder, spices and salt and mix well.
2. In another bowl, add milk, eggs, butter, sugar and pumpkin and beat until well combined.
3. Add the flour mixture and mix until just combined.
4. Add desired amount of the mixture in waffle iron and cook as suggested by the manufacturer.
5. Repeat with the remaining mixture.
6. Enjoy warm.

WEST VIRGINIA
French Toast Waffles

Prep Time: 5 mins
Total Time: 9 mins

Servings per Recipe: 2
Calories 329.3
Fat 19.2g
Cholesterol 246.3mg
Sodium 507.2mg
Carbohydrates 27.1g
Protein 11.2g

Ingredients

4 -6 slices thick-sliced bread, trimmed
2 eggs, beaten
1/4 C. milk
2 tbsp butter, melted
1/4 tsp vanilla
1/4 tsp cinnamon

Directions

1. Set your waffle iron and lightly, grease it.
2. In a shallow dish, add the butter, milk, eggs, vanilla and cinnamon and beat until well combined.
3. Coat each bread slices with egg mixture evenly.
4. Arrange the bread slices in waffle iron and cook until golden brown.
5. Enjoy warm with a topping of your favorite condiments.

Kentucky Blueberry Waffles

Prep Time: 10 mins
Total Time: 20 mins

Servings per Recipe: 1
Calories   305.7
Fat   11.9g
Cholesterol   90.8mg
Sodium   497.5mg
Carbohydrates   40.9g
Protein   8.6g

Ingredients

1 C. blueberries
3 tsp baking powder
2 eggs, separated
1 tbsp sugar
2 C. sifted flour

1 1/2 C. milk
1/2 tsp salt
1/4 C. melted butter

Directions

1. Set your waffle iron and lightly, grease it.
2. In a glass bowl, add the egg whites and beat until stiff peak form.
3. In a bowl, add the flour, baking powder and salt and mix well.
4. Now, sift the flour mixture in a second bowl.
5. In a third bowl, add the butter, egg yolks and milk and beat until well combined.
6. Slowly, add the butter mixture into the flour mixture, beating continuously until well combined.
7. Add the blueberries and gently, stir to combine.
8. Gently, fold the whipped egg whites into the flour mixture.
9. Add desired amount of the mixture in waffle iron and cook as suggested by the manufacturer.
10. Repeat with the remaining mixture.
11. Enjoy warm.

SPICED Cardamom Waffles

Prep Time: 5 mins
Total Time: 30 mins

Servings per Recipe: 4
Calories 452.3
Fat 24.8g
Cholesterol 151.9mg
Sodium 627.7mg
Carbohydrates 45.7g
Protein 11.2g

Ingredients

1 1/2 C. flour
1 1/2 tsp baking powder
3/4 tsp baking soda
1/4 tsp salt, rounded
1 tsp ground cardamom
1 C. whole milk
1 C. sour cream

1 tsp pure vanilla extract
1 tbsp mild honey
2 large eggs
3 tbsp unsalted butter, melted
powdered sugar

Directions

1. Set your waffle iron and lightly, grease it.
2. In a bowl, add the flour, baking soda, baking powder, cardamom and salt and mix well.
3. In a separate bowl, add the remaining ingredients and beat until well combined.
4. Add the flour mixture and mix until just blended.
5. Add desired amount of the mixture in waffle iron and cook as suggested by the manufacturer.
6. Repeat with the remaining mixture.
7. Enjoy with a dusting of the powdered sugar.

Sourdough Waffles

Prep Time: 5 mins
Total Time: 10 mins

Servings per Recipe: 3
Calories   247.8
Fat   11.3g
Cholesterol   62.0mg
Sodium   624.1mg
Carbohydrates   30.4g
Protein   6.8g

Ingredients

- 1/2 C. sourdough starter
- 1/2 C. whole wheat flour
- 1/2 C. any whole grain flour
- 1 C. water
- 1 egg
- 2 tbsp oil
- 1/2 tsp salt
- 1/2 tsp baking soda

Directions

1. In a bowl, add the flours, starter and water and mix until well combined.
2. With a plastic sheet, cover the bowl and keep aside for 12 hours.
3. Set your waffle iron and lightly, grease it.
4. In the bowl of the flour mixture, add the oil, salt and egg and mix until well combined.
5. Add the baking soda just before the cooking.
6. Add about 1/4 C. of the mixture in waffle iron and cook for about 5 minutes.
7. Repeat with the remaining mixture.
8. Enjoy warm.

PECAN Honey Oat Waffles

🥣 Prep Time: 10 mins
🕐 Total Time: 15 mins

Servings per Recipe: 1
Calories   247.4
Fat   13.8g
Cholesterol   51.1mg
Sodium   217.3mg
Carbohydrates   25.7g
Protein   7.5g

Ingredients

1 1/2 C. whole wheat flour
2 tsp baking powder
1/2 tsp salt
2 C. milk
2 eggs
1/4 C. melted butter
2 tbsp honey

1 C. uncooked oats
1 C. pecans, chopped

Directions

1. Set your waffle iron and lightly, grease it.
2. In a bowl, add the flour, baking powder and salt and mix well.
3. Add the butter, milk, honey and eggs and with an electric mixer, beat on medium speed until well combined.
4. Gently, fold in the oats and pecans.
5. Add desired amount of the mixture in waffle iron and cook for about 5 minutes.
6. Repeat with the remaining mixture.
7. Enjoy warm.

Moonlight Waffles

Prep Time: 9 hrs
Total Time: 9 hrs 5 mins

Servings per Recipe: 4
Calories   558.7
Fat   30.5g
Cholesterol   171.1mg
Sodium   590.2mg
Carbohydrates   56.9g
Protein   14.0g

Ingredients

- 1/2 tsp instant yeast
- 2 C. all-purpose flour
- 1 tbsp sugar
- 1/2 tsp salt
- 2 C. milk
- 8 tbsp melted butter
- 1/2 tsp vanilla
- lite olive oil
- 2 eggs, separated

Directions

1. In a bowl, add the flour, yeast, sugar and salt and mix well.
2. Add the butter, milk and vanilla and mix until well combined.
3. With a plastic wrap, cover the bowl and keep aside for the whole night.
4. In the bowl of the flour mixture, add the yolks and mix well.
5. In another bowl, add the egg whites and beat until soft peaks form.
6. Gently fold the whipped whites into the flour mixture.
7. Set your waffle iron and lightly, grease it.
8. Add desired amount of the mixture in waffle iron and cook for about 4-5 minutes.
9. Repeat with the remaining mixture.
10. Enjoy warm.

BUTTERMILK Gingerbread Waffles

Prep Time: 20 mins
Total Time: 40 mins

Servings per Recipe: 8
Calories   314.0
Fat   7.7g
Cholesterol   63.6mg
Sodium   454.1mg
Carbohydrates   55.4g
Protein   6.4g

Ingredients

4 tbsp butter, melted
2 C. flour
1 tbsp baking powder
3/4 tsp baking soda
1/4 tsp salt
1 tbsp ground ginger
3/4 tsp cinnamon

1/4 tsp ground cloves
1/4 tsp ground nutmeg
3/4 C. brown sugar
1 1/2 C. buttermilk
1/4 C. molasses
2 eggs, beaten

Directions

1. Set your waffle iron and lightly, grease it.
2. In a bowl, add the flour, baking soda, baking powder, brown sugar, spices and salt and mix well.
3. Now, sift the flour mixture into another bowl.
4. In a third bowl, add the molasses, buttermilk and egg and beat until well combined.
5. Add the melted butter and mix well.
6. Add the flour mixture and mix until just combined.
7. Add desired amount of the mixture in waffle iron and cook as suggested by the manufacturer.
8. Repeat with the remaining mixture.
9. Enjoy warm.

Kindergarten
Lunch Box Waffles

Prep Time: 5 mins
Total Time: 6 mins

Servings per Recipe: 6
Calories   692.7
Fat   34.9g
Cholesterol   205.3mg
Sodium   707.0mg
Carbohydrates   86.1g
Protein   10.1g

Ingredients

1 C. butter
4 beaten eggs
1 1/2 C. sugar
1/2 C. cocoa
2 C. flour

1 tsp vanilla
1 tsp salt
1/2 C. water

Directions

1. Set your waffle iron to medium setting and lightly, grease it.
2. In a bowl, add all the ingredients and mix until well combined.
3. Add desired amount of the mixture in waffle iron and cook for about 1 minute.
4. Repeat with the remaining mixture.
5. Enjoy warm.

CAROL'S
Cornmeal Waffles

🥣 Prep Time: 5 mins
🕐 Total Time: 25 mins

Servings per Recipe: 1
Calories   304.9
Fat   16.9g
Cholesterol   59.2mg
Sodium   368.7mg
Carbohydrates   31.6g
Protein   6.6g

Ingredients

1 egg
3/4 C. milk
1/4 C. vegetable oil
1 C. all-purpose flour
2 tbsp cornmeal

2 tsp baking powder
2 tsp sugar
1/4 tsp salt

Directions

1. Set your waffle iron and lightly, grease it.
2. In a food processor, add all the ingredients and pulse on medium-high speed until just combined.
3. Add 1/2 C. of the e mixture in waffle iron and cook for about 4-5 minutes.
4. Repeat with the remaining mixture.
5. Enjoy warm.

State Fair Waffles

🥣 Prep Time: 10 mins
🕐 Total Time: 17 mins

Servings per Recipe: 12
Calories   220.6
Fat   10.9g
Cholesterol   47.2mg
Sodium   218.1mg
Carbohydrates   27.6g
Protein   4.9g

Ingredients

2 C. all-purpose flour
1 C. semi-sweet chocolate chips
2 tsp granulated sugar
1 tbsp baking powder
1/2 tsp salt

1/2 tsp cinnamon
1 2/3 C. low-fat milk
1/3 C. unsalted butter, melted
2 extra large eggs, beaten

Directions

1. Set your waffle iron and lightly, grease it.
2. In a bowl, add the flour, sugar, chocolate chips, baking powder, cinnamon and salt and mix well.
3. Add the butter and milk and mix until well combined.
4. Add the eggs and mix until just combined.
5. Add desired amount of the mixture in waffle iron and cook as suggested by the manufacturer.
6. Repeat with the remaining mixture.
7. Enjoy warm.

3-GRAINS
Oatmeal Waffles

Prep Time: 10 mins
Total Time: 20 mins

Servings per Recipe: 15
Calories   207.8
Fat   9.5g
Cholesterol   56.4mg
Sodium   459.6mg
Carbohydrates   24.6g
Protein   6.5g

Ingredients

1 C. whole wheat flour
1 C. cornmeal
1 C. all-purpose flour
1 C. rolled oats
4 tsp baking powder
1 1/2 tsp salt
1 tsp baking soda

3 C. milk
4 eggs
6 tbsp canola oil

Directions

1. In a bowl, add the flours, cornmeal, oats, baking powder, baking soda and salt and mix well.
2. Add the remaining ingredients and mix until well combined.
3. Keep aside for about 5 minutes.
4. Add desired amount of the mixture in waffle iron and cook as suggested by the manufacturer.
5. Repeat with the remaining mixture.
6. Enjoy warm.

Mexican Hash Brown Waffles

Prep Time: 10 mins
Total Time: 30 mins

Servings per Recipe: 4
Calories   407.1
Fat   29.4g
Cholesterol   441.3mg
Sodium   1277.8mg
Carbohydrates   7.9g
Protein   27.7g

Ingredients

2 C. Simply Potatoes® Shredded Hash Browns
1 C. thick & chunky salsa, divided
8 large eggs, divided
2 C. Mexican blend cheese

8 tbsp cilantro, chopped

Directions

1. Set your waffle iron and lightly, grease it.
2. In a bowl, add the 2 eggs, potatoes and 1/3 C. of the salsa and stir until combined nicely.
3. Add the mixture in waffle iron and cook for about 15-20 minutes.
4. Meanwhile, in a bowl, crack the remaining eggs and beat well.
5. Add 1/3 C. of the salsa and stir until combined nicely.
6. For the scrambled eggs, place a nonstick wok over medium heat until heated through.
7. Add the egg mixture and until desired doneness, stirring continuously.
8. Add 1 C. of the cheese and cook, until cheese is melted, stirring continuously.
9. Remove from the heat and top with the remaining cheese evenly.
10. Cut each waffle into four equal sized pieces.
11. Divide waffle pieces onto serving plates and top each with the scrambled eggs, followed by the remaining salsa.
12. Enjoy.

HOUSTON
Waffles

🥣 Prep Time: 20 mins
🕐 Total Time: 1 hr 20 mins

Servings per Recipe: 1
Calories   213.4
Fat   7.3g
Cholesterol   77.8mg
Sodium   175.5mg
Carbohydrates   30.1g
Protein   6.6g

Ingredients

2 1/2 tsp yeast
2 C. lukewarm milk
4 eggs, separated
1 tsp vanilla
2 1/2 C. flour
1/2 tsp salt
1 tbsp sugar

1/4 C. melted butter
2 C. strawberries, hulled and sliced
1/2 C. powdered sugar

Directions

1. In a bowl, add the warm milk and yeast and mix until well combined.
2. In a second bowl, add the flour, sugar and salt and mix well.
3. In a third bowl, add the egg yolks and beat well.
4. Add the egg yolks and vanilla in the bowl of the yeast mixture and mix well.
5. Add the flour mixture and mix until just combined.
6. Add the melted butter and mix until well combined.
7. In a glass bowl, add the egg whites and beat until stiff peaks form.
8. Gently, fold the whipped egg whites into the flour mixture.
9. Keep aside in the warm area for about 45 minutes.
10. Set your waffle iron and lightly, grease it.
11. Add desired amount of the mixture in waffle iron and cook as suggested by the manufacturer.
12. Repeat with the remaining mixture.
13. Divide the waffles onto serving plates and top each with the strawberries.
14. Enjoy with a dusting of powdered sugar.

Cinnamon Pinwheel Waffles

Prep Time: 30 mins
Total Time: 50 mins

Servings per Recipe: 1
Calories   345.5
Fat   19.0g
Cholesterol   68.3mg
Sodium   306.8mg
Carbohydrates   39.8g
Protein   4.7g

Ingredients

Waffles
1 3/4 C. all-purpose flour
2 tbsp granulated sugar
1 tsp baking powder
1/2 tsp baking soda
1/4 tsp salt
2 large eggs
2 C. buttermilk
1/4 C. vegetable oil
1 tsp vanilla extract

Cinnamon Garnish
1/2 C. butter, melted
3/4 C. brown sugar, packed
1 tbsp ground cinnamon

Cheese Garnish
4 tbsp butter
2 oz. cream cheese
3/4 C. powdered sugar
1/2 tsp vanilla extract

Directions

1. For the waffles: in a bowl, add the flour, sugar, baking soda, baking powder and salt.
2. With a spoon, create a well in the middle of the flour mixture.
3. In another bowl, add the oil, buttermilk, eggs and vanilla and beat until well combined.
4. Add the egg mixture in the well of the flour mixture and mix until just combined.
5. Add desired amount of the mixture in waffle iron and cook as suggested by the manufacturer. Repeat with the remaining mixture.
6. Meanwhile, for the cinnamon topping: in a bowl, add the brown sugar, cinnamon and butter and mix until combined.
7. For the cream cheese topping: in a microwave-safe bowl, add the cream cheese and butter and microwave for about 40-60 seconds.
8. Remove from the microwave and stir until smooth.
9. Add the powdered sugar and vanilla extract and beat until well combined.
10. Divide the waffles onto serving plates and top each with the cinnamon topping, followed by the cream cheese topping. Enjoy.

BELGIAN
Waffles 101

Prep Time: 15 mins
Total Time: 50 mins

Servings per Recipe: 4
Calories   635.9
Fat   34.7g
Cholesterol   110.0mg
Sodium   750.5mg
Carbohydrates   67.2g
Protein   13.6g

Ingredients

2 C. flour
4 tsp baking powder
1/2 tsp salt
1/4 C. sugar
2 eggs
1/2 C. vegetable oil
2 C. milk
1 tsp vanilla

Directions

1. Set your waffle iron to medium-high heat and lightly, grease it.
2. In a bowl, add the flour, sugar, baking powder and salt and mix well.
3. Now, sift the flour mixture into another bowl.
4. In another bowl, add the oil, milk, egg yolks and vanilla and beat until well combined.
5. Add the flour mixture and mix until well combined.
6. In a glass bowl, add the egg whites and beat until stiff peaks form.
7. Gently, fold the whipped egg whites into the flour mixture.
8. Add desired amount of the mixture in waffle iron and cook for about 6-10 minutes.
9. Repeat with the remaining mixture.
10. Enjoy warm.

Madison Oat Waffles

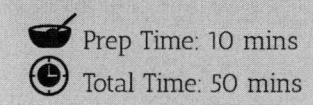

Prep Time: 10 mins
Total Time: 50 mins

Servings per Recipe: 6
Calories   200.8
Fat   8.8g
Cholesterol   28.9mg
Sodium   371.4mg
Carbohydrates   26.8g
Protein   8.4g

Ingredients

3/4 C. oat bran
1/2 C. whole wheat flour
1/2 C. all-purpose flour
2 tsp baking powder
1/2 tsp salt
1 1/2 C. skim milk
3 tbsp vegetable oil

1 egg yolk, beaten
2 egg whites

Directions

1. In a bowl, add the flours, oat bran, baking powder and salt and mix well.
2. In another bowl, add the egg yolk, oil and milk and beat until well combined.
3. Add the flour mixture and mix until just combined.
4. In a glass bowl, add the egg whites and with an electric mixer, beat on high speed until stiff peaks form.
5. Gently, fold the whipped egg whites into the flour mixture.
6. Add desired amount of the mixture in waffle iron and cook as suggested by the manufacturer.
7. Repeat with the remaining mixture.
8. Enjoy warm.

ENHANCED
Toasted Waffles

Prep Time: 1 min
Total Time: 5 mins

Servings per Recipe: 4
Calories   576.0
Fat   28.4g
Cholesterol   126.9mg
Sodium   840.8mg
Carbohydrates   68.0g
Protein   13.5g

Ingredients

8 frozen waffles, toasted
3 oz. cream cheese
14 oz. canned peaches
1 tbsp brown sugar

whipped cream

Directions

1. Spread cream cheese over each toasted waffle, followed by the fruit, brown sugar and whipped cream.
2. Enjoy.

Ice Cream Waffle Sandwiches

Prep Time: 5 mins
Total Time: 7 mins

Servings per Recipe: 1
Calories 709.7
Fat 35.6g
Cholesterol 161.5mg
Sodium 872.1mg
Carbohydrates 80.5g
Protein 16.4g

Ingredients

2 toasted hot waffles
1 C. ice cream
Toppings
1 - 2 tbsp decorative candies
1 - 2 tbsp crushed nuts
1 - 2 tbsp toasted coconut
1 - 2 tbsp granola cereal
1 - 2 tbsp praline
peanut butter spread on before ice cream

Directions

1. Place a thin layer of the peanut butter over each waffle evenly.
2. Put the ice cream onto inner part of each waffle.
3. Place your favorite topping beside the ice cream.
4. Enjoy.

COUNTRY
Cottage Waffles

Prep Time: 10 mins
Total Time: 20 mins

Servings per Recipe: 1
Calories	312.1
Fat	12.6g
Cholesterol	94.0mg
Sodium	540.3mg
Carbohydrates	38.6g
Protein	11.1g

Ingredients

4 tbsp unsalted butter, melted
1 3/4 C. all-purpose flour
2 tsp baking powder
1/4 tsp baking soda
1/2 tsp salt
1 C. cottage cheese

1 C. milk
2 large eggs
2 1/2 tbsp honey

Directions

1. Set your waffle iron and lightly, grease it.
2. In a bowl, add the flour, baking powder, baking soda and salt and mix well.
3. In another bowl, add the honey, eggs, milk and cottage cheese and beat until just combined.
4. Slowly, add the flour mixture and mix until just combined.
5. Add the butter and stir to combine.
6. Add desired amount of the mixture in waffle iron and cook as suggested by the manufacturer.
7. Repeat with the remaining mixture.
8. Enjoy warm.

Banana Waffles with Extras

Prep Time: 1 hr
Total Time: 1 hr

Servings per Recipe: 1
Calories 215.8
Fat 13.0g
Cholesterol 65.2mg
Sodium 130.1mg
Carbohydrates 22.0g
Protein 3.9g

Ingredients

1/2 C. pecans, lightly toasted
1 1/2 C. flour
1/2 C. yellow cornmeal
1 tbsp baking powder
1/4 tsp salt
1 1/4 C. milk
3/4 C. unsalted butter, melted
3 large eggs, separated
2 large ripe bananas, quartered lengthwise and chopped

3 tbsp sugar
1 tbsp light brown sugar
1 small banana, sliced into discs
maple syrup, warmed

Directions

1. Set your oven to 350 degrees F before doing anything else.
2. In the bottom of a baking sheet, place the pecans in a single layer.
3. Cook in the oven for about 10 minutes.
4. Remove from the oven and keep aside to cool completely.
5. After cooling, chop the pecans roughly. and set aside.
6. In a bowl, add the cornmeal, flour, baking powder and salt and mix well. In another bowl, add the butter, milk and egg yolks and beat until well combined.
7. Gradually, add the butter mixture into the flour mixture until just combined. Gently, fold half of the banana pieces.
8. In a glass bowl, add the egg whites and with an electric mixer, beat on medium speed until fluffy.
9. Now, beat on high speed until firm peaks form.
10. Add both sugars and beat until stiff.
11. Gently, fold the whipped egg whites into the flour mixture.

12. Set your waffle iron and lightly, grease it.
13. Add desired amount of the mixture in waffle iron and cook for about 6 minutes.
14. Repeat with the remaining mixture.
15. Enjoy warm with a topping of the banana slices, pecans and maple syrup.

Sweetened Flax Waffles

Prep Time: 20 mins
Total Time: 20 mins

Servings per Recipe: 1
Calories   125.4
Fat   5.6g
Cholesterol   38.4mg
Sodium   182.0mg
Carbohydrates 14.8g
Protein   4.5g

Ingredients

- 1 1/2 C. whole wheat flour
- 1 1/2 C. white flour
- 1/2 tsp powdered stevia
- 6 tsp baking powder
- 4 tbsp flax seeds
- 1/2 tsp salt
- 4 eggs
- 3 C. milk
- 1/4 C. olive oil

Directions

1. In a bowl, add the flours, flax seed, stevia, baking powder and salt.
2. In another bowl, add the remaining ingredients and beat until well combined.
3. Add the flour mixture and mix until just combined.
4. Add 3/4 C. of the mixture in waffle iron and cook as suggested by the manufacturer.
5. Repeat with the remaining mixture.
6. Enjoy warm.

VICTORIAN
Waffles

🥣 Prep Time: 5 mins
🕐 Total Time: 45 mins

Servings per Recipe: 1
Calories   165.2
Fat   5.7g
Cholesterol   0.0mg
Sodium   238.0mg
Carbohydrates   24.4g
Protein   4.7g

Ingredients

1 1/2 C. white flour
1 1/2 C. whole wheat flour
1/4 C. flax seed
2 tbsp sugar
1 tbsp baking powder
1 tsp salt

3 C. soy milk
1 large banana, mashed
1/4 C. canola oil
2 tsp vanilla extract

Directions

1. In a bowl, add the flours, flax seed, sugar, baking powder and salt.
2. In another bowl, add the remaining ingredients and beat until well combined.
3. Add the flour mixture and with a hand mixer, beat on a low setting well combined.
4. Heat a waffle iron and spray with oil.
5. Add desired amount of the mixture in waffle iron and cook as suggested by the manufacturer.
6. Repeat with the remaining mixture.
7. Enjoy warm.

Yam Waffles

🥣 Prep Time: 10 mins
🕐 Total Time: 40 mins

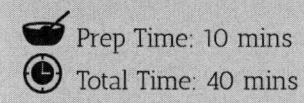

Servings per Recipe: 12
Calories   141.6
Fat   4.6g
Cholesterol   31.6mg
Sodium   157.6mg
Carbohydrates   20.7g
Protein   4.8g

Ingredients

1 C. whole wheat flour
1 C. all-purpose flour
4 tsp baking powder
1/2 tsp cinnamon
1/4 tsp clove
2 eggs, separated
1 1/2 C. skim milk

1 C. pureed cooked sweet potato
3 tbsp oil
2 tsp grated orange rind
1 tbsp granulated sugar

Directions

1. In a bowl, add the flour, spices and baking powder.
2. In another bowl, add the oil, milk, egg yolks, orange rind and sweet potato and beat until well combined.
3. Add the flour mixture and mix until just combined.
4. In a glass bowl, add the egg whites and with an electric mixer, beat until soft peaks form.
5. Add the sugar and beat until stiff peaks form.
6. Gently, fold the whipped egg whites into the flour mixture.
7. Add desired amount of the mixture in waffle iron and cook for about 5 minutes.
8. Repeat with the remaining mixture.
9. Enjoy warm.

TWIN CITY
Waffles

Prep Time: 15 mins
Total Time: 15 mins

Servings per Recipe: 4
Calories   387.0
Fat   25.0g
Cholesterol   109.0mg
Sodium   488.2mg
Carbohydrates   34.9g
Protein   6.9g

Ingredients

1 C. flour
1 1/2 tsp sugar
1 tsp baking powder
1/4 tsp baking soda
1/4 tsp salt
1 egg, separated

1 C. sour cream
1/4 C. milk
1/4 C. butter, melted
1 banana, mashed

Directions

1. Set your waffle iron and lightly, grease it.
2. In a bowl, add the flour, sugar, baking powder, baking soda and salt and mix well.
3. Now, sift the flour mixture into another bowl.
4. In another bowl, add the butter, milk, sour cream, egg yolk and banana and beat until well combined.
5. Add the flour mixture and mix until blended nicely.
6. In a glass bowl, add the egg whites and beat until stiff peak form.
7. Gently, fold the whipped egg whites into the flour mixture.
8. Add desired amount of the mixture in waffle iron and cook as suggested by the manufacturer.
9. Repeat with the remaining mixture.
10. Enjoy warm.

Light Oat Waffles

Prep Time: 10 mins
Total Time: 30 mins

Servings per Recipe: 4
Calories   213.9
Fat   8.9g
Cholesterol   0.0mg
Sodium   473.5mg
Carbohydrates   29.4g
Protein   5.2g

Ingredients

- 3/4 C. unbleached white flour
- 1/4 C. whole wheat flour
- 1/2 tsp salt
- 2 tsp baking powder
- 1/8 tsp ground cinnamon
- 1/8 tsp ground nutmeg
- 1/4 C. walnuts, chopped toasted
- 1/4 C. quick-cooking oats
- 1 1/3 C. vanilla-flavored soy milk
- 1 tbsp vegetable oil
- 1 tsp pure maple syrup

Directions

1. Set your oven to 350 degrees F before doing anything else.
2. In the bottom of a baking sheet, place the walnuts in a single layer.
3. Cook in the oven for about 5-10 minutes.
4. Remove from the oven and keep aside to cool completely.
5. In a bowl, add the flours, baking powder, spices and salt and mix well.
6. Now, sift the flour mixture into another bowl.
7. Add the oats and walnuts and stir to combine.
8. In another bowl, add the maple syrup, oil and milk and beat until well combined.
9. With a spoon, create a well in the center of the flour mixture.
10. Add the oil mixture in the well and mix until just blended.
11. Keep aside until bubbles appears on the top of the dough.
12. Set your waffle iron and lightly, grease it.
13. Add 1/3 C. of the mixture in waffle iron and cook as suggested by the manufacturer.
14. Repeat with the remaining mixture.
15. Enjoy warm.

VEGAN
Almond Waffles

Prep Time: 5 mins
Total Time: 10 mins

Servings per Recipe: 6
Calories	299.6
Fat	25.4g
Cholesterol	0.0mg
Sodium	414.4mg
Carbohydrates	15.6g
Protein	5.0g

Ingredients

1 large banana, mashed
1 3/4 C. soy milk
1/2 C. vegetable oil
1 tbsp honey
2 C. gluten-free flour
4 tsp baking powder
1/4 tsp salt
1/2 C. chopped almonds

Directions

1. Set your waffle iron and lightly, grease it.
2. In a bowl, add the oil, soy milk, honey and bananas and with an electric mixer, beat until well combined.
3. Add the baking powder, flour and salt and mix until just combined.
4. Gently, fold in the almonds.
5. Set your waffle iron and lightly, grease it.
6. Add 2/3 C. of the mixture in waffle iron and cook for about 5 minutes.
7. Repeat with the remaining mixture.
8. Enjoy warm.

Crispy Waffles 101

Prep Time: 15 mins
Total Time: 22 mins

Servings per Recipe: 1
Calories   148.5
Fat   7.0g
Cholesterol   24.5mg
Sodium   135.8mg
Carbohydrates   17.4g
Protein   3.6g

Ingredients

2 eggs, beaten
1 tsp salt
1 tbsp sugar
1/2 C. vegetable oil
2 C. warm milk
1 (1/4 oz.) package yeast, dissolved in 1/4 C. water
3 1/4 C. flour, sifted

Directions

1. In a bowl, add the oil, eggs, sugar and salt and mix well.
2. In another bowl, add the flour, yeast mixture and warm milk and mix until well combined.
3. With a plastic wrap, cover the bowl and place in the fridge for whole night.
4. Set your waffle iron and lightly, grease it.
5. Add desired amount of the mixture in waffle iron and cook as suggested by the manufacturer.
6. Repeat with the remaining mixture.
7. Enjoy warm.

HOW TO
Make a Liege Waffle

🥣 Prep Time: 30 mins
🕐 Total Time: 35 mins

Servings per Recipe: 4
Calories 904.4
Fat 50.3g
Cholesterol 261.5mg
Sodium 534.2mg
Carbohydrates 103.3g
Protein 12.2g

Ingredients

1 (1/4 oz.) package yeast
1/3 C. lukewarm water
1 1/2 tbsp granulated sugar
1/8 tsp salt
2 C. flour
3 eggs

1 C. softened butter
1 C. pearl sugar

Directions

1. In a bowl, add the sugar, yeast, salt and water and mix until well combined.
2. Keep aside for about 13-15 minutes.
3. In another bowl, add the flour and with a spoon, create a well in the center.
4. Add the yeast mixture in the center with your hands, knead until well combined.
5. Slowly, add the eggs, 1 at a time alongside 2 tbsp of the butter and mix well.
6. Keep aside in warm place until dough rises in bulk.
7. Add the pearl sugar and gently, stir to combine.
8. Keep aside for about 13-15 minutes.
9. Set your waffle iron and lightly, grease it.
10. Add 3 tbsp of the dough of in waffle iron and cook for about 4-5 minutes.
11. Repeat with the remaining mixture.
12. Enjoy warm.

July's Zesty Waffles

Prep Time: 50 mins
Total Time: 1 hr 5 mins

Servings per Recipe: 1
Calories   308.3
Fat   11.9g
Cholesterol   131.7mg
Sodium   442.8mg
Carbohydrates   41.6g
Protein   9.5g

Ingredients

1 3/4 C. all-purpose flour, sifted
2 tsp baking powder
1/2 tsp baking soda
1/4 tsp salt
1 lemon, zest, grated

1 3/4 C. low-fat milk
1/4 C. melted butter
3 eggs, separated
2 tbsp icing sugar

Directions

1. In a bowl, add the flour, baking soda, baking powder and salt and mix well.
2. Now, sift the flour mixture into another bowl.
3. Add the lemon zest and mix well.
4. In another bowl, add the egg yolks, butter and milk and beat until well combined.
5. With a spoon, create a well in the center of the flour mixture.
6. Slowly, add the flour mixture in the well and mix until just blended.
7. With a plastic sheet, cover the bowl and
8. keep aside for about 30 minutes.
9. Set your waffle iron and lightly, grease it.
10. In a glass bowl, add the egg whites and beat until fluffy.
11. Slowly, add the icing sugar, beating continuously until soft peaks form.
12. Gently, fold the whipped egg whites into the flour mixture.
13. Add desired amount of the mixture in waffle iron and cook as suggested by the manufacturer.
14. Repeat with the remaining mixture.
15. Enjoy warm.

APPLE, WALNUTS, and Pumpkin Waffles

Prep Time: 10 mins
Total Time: 40 mins

Servings per Recipe: 6
Calories 249.5
Fat 8.9g
Cholesterol 36.9mg
Sodium 301.7mg
Carbohydrates 33.7g
Protein 8.5g

Ingredients

1 large egg, beaten
2 egg whites, beaten
4 tbsp brown sugar
1 C. evaporated skim milk
2 tbsp vegetable oil
1/2 C. pumpkin puree, canned
2 tsp vanilla
1 C. all-purpose flour
2 tsp baking powder
1/4 tsp salt

1 1/2 tsp cinnamon
1/2 tsp nutmeg
1/4 tsp ginger
1/4 tsp clove
1/2 C. apple, diced
1/4 C. toasted walnuts

Directions

1. Set your waffle iron and lightly, grease it.
2. In a bowl, add the flour, baking powder and salt and mix well.
3. In another bowl, add the pumpkin, sugar, oil, milk, egg, egg whites and vanilla and beat until well combined.
4. Add the flour mixture and mix until just combined.
5. Gently, fold in the walnuts and apple.
6. Add 3/4 C. of the mixture in waffle iron and cook as suggested by the manufacturer.
7. Repeat with the remaining mixture.
8. Enjoy warm.

Florida Duplex Waffles with Vanilla Syrup

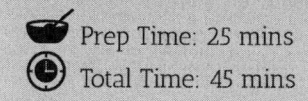

🥣 Prep Time: 25 mins
🕐 Total Time: 45 mins

Servings per Recipe: 8
Calories   429.2
Fat   12.5g
Cholesterol   83.4mg
Sodium   325.8mg
Carbohydrates   72.0g
Protein   8.8g

Ingredients

2 C. all-purpose flour
1 tbsp sugar
2 tsp baking powder
1/2 tsp salt
3 eggs, separated
2 C. milk
1/4 C. vegetable oil
Syrup
1 C. sugar

1/2 C. light corn syrup
1/4 C. water
1 (5 oz.) cans evaporated milk
1 tsp vanilla extract
1/2 tsp ground cinnamon

Directions

1. In a bowl, add the sugar, flour, baking powder and salt.
2. Add the oil, milk and egg yolks and mix until just combined.
3. In a glass bowl, add the egg whites and beat until stiff peak form.
4. Gently, fold the whipped egg whites into the flour mixture.
5. Add desired amount of the mixture in waffle iron and cook as suggested by the manufacturer.
6. Repeat with the remaining mixture.
7. In the meantime, for the syrup: in a pot, add the corn syrup, sugar and water over medium heat and cook until boiling.
8. Cook for until desired thickness of the syrup.
9. Remove from the heat and immediately, stir in the milk, cinnamon and vanilla.
10. Enjoy the waffles alongside the syrup.

WAFFLES
Stockholm

Prep Time: 10 mins
Total Time: 25 mins

Servings per Recipe: 2
Calories   894.4
Fat   45.4g
Cholesterol   505.7mg
Sodium   308.5mg
Carbohydrates   100.8g
Protein   21.7g

Ingredients

4 eggs
100 g sugar
120 g flour
200 ml sour cream

3 tbsp butter, melted
1 tsp ground cardamom

Directions

1. In a bowl, add the sugar and eggs and beat until fluffy.
2. Add the sour cream, flour and cardamom and mix until well combined.
3. Add the butter and mix well.
4. Keep aside for about 15 minutes.
5. Set your waffle iron and lightly, grease it.
6. Add desired amount of the mixture in waffle iron and cook as suggested by the manufacturer.
7. Repeat with the remaining mixture.
8. Enjoy warm.

Gingery Pumpkin Waffles

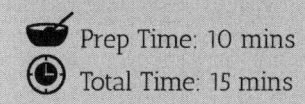

🥣 Prep Time: 10 mins
🕐 Total Time: 15 mins

Servings per Recipe: 4
Calories 585.5
Fat 18.5g
Cholesterol 222.6mg
Sodium 1053.9mg
Carbohydrates 84.7g
Protein 19.9g

Ingredients

2 1/2 C. all-purpose flour
1/4 C. brown sugar
2 tsp baking powder
1 tsp baking soda
1/2 tsp kosher salt
2 tsp ground cinnamon
1 tsp ground ginger
1/2 tsp ground cloves
4 large eggs

2 1/2 C. shaken buttermilk
4 tbsp melted butter
1 C. pumpkin puree
Confectioners' sugar

Directions

1. Set your waffle iron and lightly, grease it.
2. In a bowl, add the flour, brown sugar, baking soda, baking powder, spices and salt and mix well.
3. Now, sift the flour mixture into a second bowl.
4. In a third bowl, add the butter, buttermilk, eggs and pumpkin and beat until well combined.
5. Add the flour mixture and mix until blended nicely.
6. Add desired amount of the mixture in waffle iron and cook as suggested by the manufacturer.
7. Repeat with the remaining mixture.
8. Enjoy warm with a dusting of the confectioners' sugar.

WILLIE MAE'S
Buttermilk Waffles

Prep Time: 10 mins
Total Time: 25 mins

Servings per Recipe: 4
Calories   176.9
Fat   4.5g
Cholesterol   2.4mg
Sodium   700.1mg
Carbohydrates   26.8g
Protein   6.8g

Ingredients

3/4 C. all-purpose flour
1/4 C. cornmeal
1 tsp baking soda
1/2 tsp salt
1 C. buttermilk
1 tbsp canola oil

2 egg whites
1 tbsp vanilla
1/2 C. wheat germ

Directions

1. Set your waffle iron and lightly, grease it.
2. In a bowl, add the flour, cornmeal, baking soda and salt and mix well.
3. In another bowl, add the oil, buttermilk and vanilla and beat until well combined.
4. Add the flour mixture and mix until well combined.
5. In a glass bowl, add the egg whites and beat until stiff peak form.
6. Gently, fold the whipped egg whites into the flour mixture.
7. Add desired amount of the mixture in waffle iron and cook as suggested by the manufacturer.
8. Repeat with the remaining mixture.
9. Enjoy warm.

Rochester
Lemon Waffles

Prep Time: 30 mins
Total Time: 45 mins

Servings per Recipe: 1
Calories   309.7
Fat   19.4g
Cholesterol   195.2mg
Sodium   157.8mg
Carbohydrates   25.7g
Protein   8.2g

Ingredients

5 eggs
1/4 C. sugar
1 C. flour, sifted
1 tsp lemon juice,
1/2 tsp lemon peel, grated

1 C. sour cream
1/4 C. butter

Directions

1. In a bowl, add the sugar and eggs and beat until mixture becomes fluffy.
2. Add the flour, sour cream and lemon peel and mix until well combined.
3. Add the lemon juice and butter and mix until well combined.
4. Keep aside for about 12-15 minutes.
5. Set your waffle iron and lightly, grease it.
6. Add 3/4 C. of the mixture in waffle iron and cook for about 50-60 seconds per side.
7. Repeat with the remaining mixture.
8. Enjoy warm.

SPELMAN
Seltzer Waffles

Prep Time: 5 mins
Total Time: 15 mins

Servings per Recipe: 1
Calories   65.6
Fat   6.0g
Cholesterol   33.8mg
Sodium   164.1mg
Carbohydrates   1.2g
Protein   1.7g

Ingredients

2 1/4 C. spelt flour
1 tbsp baking powder
1/4 tsp salt
2 eggs
1 C. milk

3/4 C. seltzer water
1/4 C. oil

Directions

1. Set your waffle iron and lightly, grease it.
2. In a bowl, add the flour, baking powder and salt and mix well.
3. Add the remaining ingredients and mix until well combined.
4. Add desired amount of the mixture in waffle iron and cook for about 3-5 minutes.
5. Repeat with the remaining mixture.
6. Enjoy warm.

London Butterscotch Waffles

Prep Time: 1 hr
Total Time: 1 hr

Servings per Recipe: 6
Calories 480.6
Fat 14.0g
Cholesterol 113.8mg
Sodium 426.7mg
Carbohydrates 77.0g
Protein 11.6g

Ingredients

2 1/4 C. flour
1/2 tsp baking powder
1/2 tsp baking soda
1/2 tsp salt
1 tsp cinnamon
1/2 tsp nutmeg
1/4 C. brown sugar, packed

3 eggs, separated
2 C. sour milk
2 ripe bananas, mashed well
1 C. butterscotch chips

Directions

1. In a bowl, add the flour, brown sugar, baking soda, baking powder, spices and salt and mix well.
2. Now, sift the flour mixture into another bowl.
3. In a separate bowl, add the egg yolks and beat.
4. Add the bananas and sour milk and beat until well combined.
5. Add the flour mixture and mix until combined nicely.
6. In a glass bowl, add the egg whites and beat until stiff peak form.
7. Gently, fold the whipped egg whites into the flour mixture.
8. Now, gently fold in the butterscotch chips.
9. Set your waffle iron and lightly, grease it.
10. Add desired amount of the mixture in waffle iron and cook as suggested by the manufacturer.
11. Repeat with the remaining mixture.
12. Enjoy warm.

WAFFLES
Augusta Autumn

Prep Time: 5 mins
Total Time: 25 mins

Servings per Recipe: 4
Calories   413.1
Fat   10.8g
Cholesterol   163.7mg
Sodium   600.0mg
Carbohydrates   65.1g
Protein   14.1g

Ingredients

1 3/4 C. flour
2 tsp baking powder
3 tsp sugar
1/2 tsp salt
3 eggs, separated

1 1/2 C. milk
1/3 C. applesauce
1 C. whipped cream
1 C. canned peaches in light syrup

Directions

1. Set your waffle iron and lightly, grease it.
2. In a bowl add the flour, sugar, baking powder and salt and mix well.
3. In another bowl, add the milk and egg yolks and beat until blended nicely.
4. Add the flour mixture and mix until well combined.
5. Add the applesauce and mix until well combined.
6. In a glass bowl, add the egg whites and beat until stiff peak form.
7. Gently, fold the whipped egg whites into the flour mixture.
8. Add 2/3 C. of the mixture in waffle iron and cook for about 3-4 minutes.
9. Repeat with the remaining mixture.
10. Enjoy warm with a topping of the peach slices and whipped cream.

Corn on Oats Waffles

Prep Time: 10 mins
Total Time: 40 mins

Servings per Recipe: 4
Calories   531.7
Fat   19.9g
Cholesterol   93.6mg
Sodium   871.7mg
Carbohydrates   73.9g
Protein   14.8g

Ingredients

1 large egg
2 2/3 C. buttermilk
1 1/3 C. unbleached all-purpose flour
2/3 C. regular rolled oats
2/3 C. cornmeal
1 1/4 tsp baking soda
1/4 tsp salt

3 tbsp sugar
1/3 C. melted butter, cooled

Directions

1. In a bowl, add the flour, oats, cornmeal, baking soda, sugar and salt and mix well.
2. In another bowl, crack the egg and beat.
3. Add the buttermilk and beat until well combined.
4. Add the flour mixture and mix until just combined.
5. Add the butter and stir until just combined.
6. Add 2/3 C. of the mixture in waffle iron and cook as suggested by the manufacturer.
7. Repeat with the remaining mixture.
8. Enjoy warm.

COFFEE
Bisquick Waffles

Prep Time: 15 mins
Total Time: 30 mins

Servings per Recipe: 4
Calories   459.5
Fat   24.1g
Cholesterol   53.8mg
Sodium   694.0mg
Carbohydrates   52.9g
Protein   9.2g

Ingredients

1 (1/8 oz.) packet instant coffee
1/3 C. hot water
2 C. baking mix (Bisquick)
1/3 C. miniature chocolate chip
1 C. whole milk

1 large egg
2 tbsp vegetable oil
syrup
1/4 C. miniature chocolate chip

Directions

1. Set your waffle iron and lightly, grease it.
2. In a bowl, add the coffee packet and 1/3 C. of the hot water and mix until well combined.
3. Add the chocolate morsels, baking mix, egg, oil and milk and beat until blended nicely.
4. Add desired amount of the mixture in waffle iron and cook as suggested by the manufacturer.
5. Repeat with the remaining mixture.
6. Enjoy warm with a topping of the chocolate morsels.

Poppy Seed Waffles

Prep Time: 20 mins
Total Time: 30 mins

Servings per Recipe: 4
Calories   661.8
Fat   18.2g
Cholesterol   173.0mg
Sodium   736.1mg
Carbohydrates   115.0g
Protein   13.5g

Ingredients

Berry Glaze
1 lb. frozen blueberries, thawed and undrained
6 tbsp apple juice
1/2 C. sugar
1 tbsp cornstarch
1 tbsp lemon juice
Waffles
1 1/2 C. all-purpose flour
6 tbsp sugar

2 tbsp poppy seeds
1 1/2 tsp baking powder
1 tsp baking soda
1/4 tsp salt
3 large eggs
1 1/4 C. buttermilk
1/4 C. unsalted butter, melted
1 tbsp grated lemon, rind

Directions

1. For the sauce: in a heavy-bottomed pan, add the sugar, blueberries and 1/2 C. of the apple juice over medium heat and cook until boiling. Cook for about 14-15 minutes, stirring occasionally.
2. In a bowl, add the remaining 2 tbsp of the apple juice and 1 tbsp of the cornstarch and mix until well combined.
3. Add the cornstarch mixture into the blueberry mixture and stir to combine. Stir in the lemon juice and cook until boiling, mixing continuously. Cook for about 1 minute.
4. Remove from the heat and keep aside to cool.
5. For the waffles: in a bowl, add the flour, sugar, poppy seeds, baking powder, baking soda and salt and mix well.
6. In another bowl, add the butter, buttermilk, eggs and lemon peel and beat until well combined.
7. Add the flour mixture and mix until just combined.
8. Keep aside for about 13-15 minutes.

9. Add desired amount of the mixture in waffle iron and cook for about 7 minutes.
10. Repeat with the remaining mixture.
11. Enjoy warm with a topping of the blueberry sauce.

Citrus Waffles

Prep Time: 10 mins
Total Time: 20 mins

Servings per Recipe: 4
Calories   466.7
Fat   18.2g
Cholesterol   246.3mg
Sodium   731.4mg
Carbohydrates   60.9g
Protein   14.1g

Ingredients

2 C. flour
3 tsp baking powder
2 tbsp sugar
1/2 tsp salt
4 eggs
1/2 C. milk
1/2 C. pulp free orange juice
4 tbsp melted butter
3 tbsp grated orange zest

Directions

1. Set your waffle iron and lightly, grease it.
2. In a bowl, add the flour, sugar, baking powder and salt and mix well.
3. Now, sift the flour mixture into another bowl.
4. In another bowl, add the eggs, butter, milk and orange juice and beat until well combined.
5. Add the orange zest and stir to combine.
6. Add the flour mixture and mix until well combined.
7. Add desired amount of the mixture in waffle iron and cook as suggested by the manufacturer.
8. Repeat with the remaining mixture.
9. Enjoy warm.

CHOCO CHIP
Waffles

🥣 Prep Time: 5 mins
🕐 Total Time: 15 mins

Servings per Recipe: 8
Calories   321.2
Fat   15.4g
Cholesterol   49.0mg
Sodium   323.6mg
Carbohydrates   40.3g
Protein   7.1g

Ingredients

2 C. all-purpose flour
2 tbsp sugar
1 tbsp baking powder
1/2 tsp salt
1 2/3-2 C. low-fat milk

1 medium banana, mashed
6 tbsp vegetable oil
2 large eggs
1/2 C. mini chocolate chip

Directions

1. In a bowl, add the flour, sugar, baking powder and salt and mix well.
2. Add the remaining ingredients and mix until combined nicely.
3. Keep aside for about 4-5 minutes before cooking.
4. Set your waffle iron and lightly, grease it.
5. Add 1/2 C. of the mixture in waffle iron and cook for about 2 minutes.
6. Repeat with the remaining mixture.
7. Enjoy warm.

Hudson Valley
Fruit Waffle Pudding

Prep Time: 10 mins
Total Time: 45 mins

Servings per Recipe: 6
Calories   1003.1
Fat   61.0g
Cholesterol   308.2mg
Sodium   861.2mg
Carbohydrates   96.5g
Protein   19.6g

Ingredients

12 waffles, cubed
300 g raspberries,
200 g white chocolate, chopped
1/4 C. caster sugar
1 tbsp plain flour
3 eggs
1 tsp grated lemon rind
1 tsp vanilla extract
500 ml thickened cream
2 tbsp icing sugar

Directions

1. Set your oven to 350 degrees F before doing anything else and grease a baking dish.
2. In a bowl, add the flour, sugar, lemon rind, cream, eggs and vanilla and beat until well combined.
3. In the bottom of the prepared baking dish, arrange half of the waffles.
4. Place half of raspberries over the waffles evenly, followed by half of the chocolate.
5. Repeat the layers once and top with the egg mixture evenly.
6. Keep aside for about 10-12 minutes.
7. Cook in the oven for about 35 minutes.
8. Enjoy with a dusting of the icing sugar.

TEX-MEX Cornbread Waffles

Prep Time: 15 mins
Total Time: 19 mins

Servings per Recipe: 9
Calories   237.7
Fat   10.8g
Cholesterol   52.6mg
Sodium   358.6mg
Carbohydrates   28.1g
Protein   7.7g

Ingredients

1 C. cornmeal
1 C. all-purpose flour
2 1/2 tsp baking powder
1 tsp xanthan gum
1 tbsp sugar
1 tsp cumin
1/4 tsp baking soda
1/2 tsp salt
5 tbsp dry buttermilk
1 1/4-1 1/2 C. water

1/4 C. vegetable oil
2 large eggs, separated
1 medium ear corn on the cob, kernels cut off
2/3 C. grated sharp cheddar cheese
1 -2 medium jalapeño peppers, diced

Directions

1. Set your waffle iron and lightly, grease it.
2. In a bowl, add the cornmeal, flour, xanthan gum, sugar, buttermilk powder, baking powder, baking soda, cumin and salt and mix until well combined.
3. In another bowl, add the egg yolks, oil and 1 1/4 C. of the warm water and beat until well combined.
4. Add the flour mixture and mix until well combined.
5. Add the cheese, corn and peppers and gently, stir to combine.
6. In a glass bowl, add the egg whites and beat until stiff peaks form.
7. Gently, fold the whipped egg whites into the flour mixture.
8. Add desired amount of the mixture in waffle iron and cook as suggested by the manufacturer.
9. Repeat with the remaining mixture.
10. Enjoy warm.

Strawberry Waffles

Prep Time: 15 mins
Total Time: 20 mins

Servings per Recipe: 3
Calories	228.1
Fat	4.4g
Cholesterol	70.9mg
Sodium	256.7mg
Carbohydrates	39.2g
Protein	9.0g

Ingredients

1/2 C. whole wheat flour
1/2 C. all-purpose flour
2 tbsp ground flax seeds
2 tsp sugar substitute
1 tsp baking powder
1/8 tsp salt
1 C. sliced strawberry
1/4 C. skim milk
2 tbsp natural applesauce
1/2 tsp vanilla extract
1 large egg

Directions

1. Set your waffle iron and lightly, grease it.
2. In a bowl, add the flax seed, flours, Splenda, baking powder and salt and mix well.
3. With a spoon, create a well in the middle of the flour mixture.
4. In a food processor, add the strawberries, egg, applesauce, milk and vanilla and pulse until pureed.
5. Add the pureed mixture into the well of the flour mixture and mix until just combined.
6. Add 1/2 C. of the mixture in waffle iron and cook for about 5 minutes.
7. Repeat with the remaining mixture.
8. Enjoy warm.

AMERICAN
Applesauce Waffles

🥣 Prep Time: 5 mins
🕐 Total Time: 10 mins

Servings per Recipe: 8
Calories   345.5
Fat   4.3g
Cholesterol   110.3mg
Sodium   223.8mg
Carbohydrates   64.6g
Protein   13.6g

Ingredients

- 3/4 C. applesauce
- 2 C. unbleached all-purpose flour
- 2 C. whole wheat flour
- 3 tsp baking powder
- 4 tbsp brown sugar
- 1 tsp ground cinnamon
- 1/4 tsp ground cloves
- 1/4 tsp ground nutmeg
- 4 eggs
- 3 C. low-fat milk
- 1/2 C. apple juice
- 2 tbsp ginger, grated

Directions

1. Set your waffle iron and lightly, grease it.
2. In a bowl, add the flours, sugar, baking powder and spices and mix well.
3. In a separate bowl, add the remaining ingredients and beat until well combined.
4. Add the flour mixture and mix until just combined.
5. Add desired amount of the mixture in waffle iron and cook as suggested by the manufacturer.
6. Repeat with the remaining mixture.
7. Enjoy warm.

Peanut Butter Waffles

Prep Time: 15 mins
Total Time: 20 mins

Servings per Recipe: 6
Calories   453.1
Fat   25.6g
Cholesterol   71.1mg
Sodium   477.3mg
Carbohydrates   44.9g
Protein   16.3g

Ingredients

2 1/4 C. whole wheat flour
4 tsp baking powder
1/2 C. creamy peanut butter
1 1/2 tbsp sugar
2 eggs, beaten
2 1/4 C. whole milk
1/4 C. vegetable oil
1/4 tsp kosher salt
cooking spray

Directions

1. Set your waffle iron and lightly, grease it with the cooking spray.
2. In the bowl of an electric mixer, fitted with the paddle attachment, add the remaining ingredients and mix until well combined.
3. Add desired amount of the mixture in waffle iron and cook for about 4-5 minutes.
4. Repeat with the remaining mixture.
5. Enjoy warm.

MARGARITA'S
Meringue Waffles

Prep Time: 20 mins
Total Time: 40 mins

Servings per Recipe: 6
Calories 248.8
Fat 7.8g
Cholesterol 56.3mg
Sodium 350.1mg
Carbohydrates 35.7g
Protein 8.0g

Ingredients

Waffle
2 C. plain flour
1/2 tsp baking soda
1/2 tsp salt
2 tbsp extra granulated sugar
1 egg, separated
1 1/4 C. milk
1/8 C. unsalted butter, melted

2 tsp grated lemon zest
Garnish
12 tbsp yogurt
12 tbsp lemon curd
12 small meringues, crushed
mint leaf

Directions

1. Set your waffle iron and lightly, grease it.
2. In a bowl, add the flour, sugar, baking soda, salt and mix well.
3. With a spoon, create a well in the middle of the flour mixture.
4. Add the milk and egg yolk in the well of the flour mixture and with a whisk, mix until well combined
5. Add the butter and lemon zest and gently, stir to combine.
6. In a glass bowl, add the egg whites and beat until stiff peaks form.
7. Gently, fold the whipped egg whites into the flour mixture.
8. Add desired amount of the mixture in waffle iron and cook as suggested by the manufacturer.
9. Repeat with the remaining mixture.
10. Meanwhile, for the topping: in a bowl, add the lemon curd and yogurt and stir to combine.
11. Divide the waffles onto serving plates.
12. Place a dollop of the yogurt mixture over each waffle.
13. Enjoy with a topping of the meringue and mint leaves.

Simply Grated Waffles

🥣 Prep Time: 15 mins
🕐 Total Time: 35 mins

Servings per Recipe: 4
Calories 413.0
Fat 15.1g
Cholesterol 140.7mg
Sodium 904.7mg
Carbohydrates 53.7g
Protein 14.9g

Ingredients

2 C. flour
4 tsp baking powder
1/2 tsp salt
2 eggs
1 1/4 C. milk

2 tbsp melted butter
1/2 C. of grated cheese

Directions

1. Set your waffle iron and lightly, grease it.
2. In a bowl, sift together the flour, baking powder and salt.
3. In another bowl, add the milk and egg yolks and beat well.
4. In the bowl of the flour mixture, add the milk mixture, and mix well.
5. Add the butter and mix well.
6. Add the cheese and gently, stir to combine.
7. In a glass bowl, add the egg whites and beat until stiff peaks form.
8. Gently, fold the whipped egg whites into the flour mixture.
9. Add desired amount of the mixture in waffle iron and cook as suggested by the manufacturer.
10. Repeat with the remaining mixture.
11. Enjoy warm.

BRAZILIAN
Banana Waffles

🥣 Prep Time: 5 mins
🕐 Total Time: 20 mins

Servings per Recipe: 4
Calories   558.1
Fat   33.3g
Cholesterol   95.8mg
Sodium   494.9mg
Carbohydrates   53.5g
Protein   11.9g

Ingredients

1 3/4 C. all-purpose flour
1 tbsp baking powder
1 tsp ground cinnamon
1/4 tsp nutmeg
1/4 tsp salt
2 egg yolks
1 1/2 C. milk
2/3 C. banana, ripened and mashed

1/2 C. cooking oil
2 egg whites

Directions

1. In a bowl, add the flour, spices, baking powder and salt and mix well.
2. In another bowl, add the oil, milk, egg yolks and banana and beat until well combined.
3. Slowly, add the flour mixture and mix until just combined.
4. In a glass bowl, add the egg whites and beat until stiff peaks form.
5. Gently, fold the whipped egg whites into the flour mixture.
6. Add 1-1 1/4 C. of the mixture in waffle iron and cook as suggested by the manufacturer.
7. Repeat with the remaining mixture.
8. Enjoy warm.

Arizona Waffles

Prep Time: 8 mins
Total Time: 16 mins

Servings per Recipe: 4
Calories   746.5
Fat   43.4g
Cholesterol   153.4mg
Sodium   1338.1mg
Carbohydrates   68.7g
Protein   26.9g

Ingredients

- 1 1/2 C. all-purpose flour
- 1/2 C. yellow cornmeal
- 1 1/3 C. longhorn cheese, grated
- 1 tbsp baking powder
- 2 tsp sugar
- 1/2 tsp salt
- 1 tsp mild chili powder
- 1 2/3 C. milk
- 2 eggs, beaten
- 1/3 C. vegetable oil
- 2 tbsp chopped green chilies

Directions

1. Set your waffle iron and lightly, grease it.
2. In a bowl, add the cheese, cornmeal, flour, sugar, baking powder, chili powder and salt and mix well
3. Add the eggs, oil, milk and chilies and beat until just combined.
4. Add desired amount of the mixture in waffle iron and cook as suggested by the manufacturer.
5. Repeat with the remaining mixture.
6. Enjoy warm.

10-MINUTE
College Waffles

Prep Time: 5 mins
Total Time: 10 mins

Servings per Recipe: 4
Calories   516.0
Fat   37.7g
Cholesterol   54.0mg
Sodium   799.6mg
Carbohydrates   38.0g
Protein   6.3g

Ingredients

2 C. Bisquick
1 1/3 C. club soda
1 egg
1/2 C. oil

Directions

1. Set your waffle iron and lightly, grease it.
2. In a bowl, add all the ingredients and mix until well combined.
3. Add desired amount of the mixture in waffle iron and cook as suggested by the manufacturer.
4. Repeat with the remaining mixture.
5. Enjoy warm.

Waffles in Norway

Prep Time: 15 mins
Total Time: 25 mins

Servings per Recipe: 8
Calories   276.3
Fat   13.8g
Cholesterol   100.8mg
Sodium   251.7mg
Carbohydrates   32.3g
Protein   6.0g

Ingredients

- 3 eggs, lightly beaten
- 1/2 C. sugar
- 1 (16 oz.) containers sour cream
- 1 1/2 C. flour
- 1 pinch salt
- 1 tsp baking soda
- 1/2 tsp ground cardamom
- strawberry jam

Directions

1. In a bowl, add the sugar and eggs and beat until fluffy.
2. Add the remaining ingredients and mix until just combined.
3. Keep aside for about 9-10 minutes.
4. Set your waffle iron and lightly, grease it.
5. Add desired amount of the mixture in waffle iron and cook as suggested by the manufacturer.
6. Repeat with the remaining mixture.
7. Enjoy warm with a topping of the strawberry jam.

RASPBERRY
Fall Waffles

Prep Time: 8 mins
Total Time: 18 mins

Servings per Recipe: 12
Calories	171.2
Fat	6.5g
Cholesterol	39.5mg
Sodium	203.7mg
Carbohydrates	24.2g
Protein	3.9g

Ingredients

1 1/2 C. all-purpose flour
1 tbsp sugar
2 1/2 tsp baking powder
1/2 tsp salt
2 eggs
1 1/2 C. milk

2 tbsp vegetable oil
1/2 C. raspberry preserves
1/3 C. chopped pecans

Directions

1. In a microwave-safe bowl, add the raspberry preserves and microwave for about 1 minute.
2. In a bowl, add the flour, baking powder, sugar and salt and mix well.
3. In another bowl, add the oil, milk and eggs and beat until well combined.
4. Add the flour mixture and mix until just combined.
5. Gently, fold in the warm raspberry preserves and pecans and mix until just blended.
6. Add desired amount of the mixture in waffle iron and cook as suggested by the manufacturer.
7. Repeat with the remaining mixture.
8. Enjoy warm.

Rye Waffles

Prep Time: 30 mins
Total Time: 30 mins

Servings per Recipe: 1
Calories   2558.3
Fat   129.7g
Cholesterol   684.3mg
Sodium   5297.5mg
Carbohydrates   304.1g
Protein   60.5g

Ingredients

- 2 C. milk
- 1 tbsp lemon juice
- 2 eggs
- 2 tsp sugar
- 2 C. cornmeal
- 1 C. rye flour
- 1/2 C. butter, melted
- 2 tbsp baking powder
- 1 tsp baking soda
- 1/4 tsp salt

Directions

1. In a bowl, add the cornmeal, rye, sugar, eggs and butter and mix until well combined.
2. Keep aside for about 14-15 minutes.
3. Set your waffle iron and lightly, grease it.
4. Add the lemon juice and mix well.
5. Add the baking powder and baking soda and mix well.
6. Add desired amount of the mixture in waffle iron and cook as suggested by the manufacturer.
7. Repeat with the remaining mixture.
8. Enjoy warm.

OATMEAL Waffles

Prep Time: 15 mins
Total Time: 35 mins

Servings per Recipe: 6
Calories 397.6
Fat 19.0g
Cholesterol 113.6mg
Sodium 602.4mg
Carbohydrates 48.1g
Protein 10.5g

Ingredients

1 C. oatmeal
2 tbsp toasted wheat germ
1/2 C. butter, melted
2 eggs, beaten
1/4 C. honey
1 C. all-purpose flour
1/2 C. whole wheat flour
1 tsp baking soda
1/2 tsp salt
1 1/2 C. buttermilk
butter
syrup

Directions

1. Set your waffle iron and lightly, grease it.
2. In a bowl, add the wheat germ and cereal and mix well.
3. In a second bowl, add the flours, salt and baking soda and mix well.
4. In a third bowl, add the honey, eggs and butter and beat until well combined.
5. Add the cereal mixture and mix well.
6. Add the flour mixture, alternating with the buttermilk and mix until a very stiff mixture is formed.
7. Add desired amount of the mixture in waffle iron and cook as suggested by the manufacturer.
8. Repeat with the remaining mixture.
9. Enjoy warm with a topping of the butter and syrup.

Belgian Fruit Waffles

Prep Time: 10 mins
Total Time: 20 mins

Servings per Recipe: 6
Calories   375.5
Fat   13.8g
Cholesterol   103.2mg
Sodium   431.5mg
Carbohydrates   54.9g
Protein   8.2g

Ingredients

- 1/3 C. butter
- 1/2 C. sugar
- 2 large eggs
- 2 C. flour
- 2 tsp baking powder
- 1/2 tsp salt
- 1 C. milk
- 1 1/2 C. sliced peaches, chopped
- 1/2 tsp vanilla
- 1/2 tsp lemon juice

Directions

1. Set your waffle iron and lightly, grease it.
2. In a glass bowl, add the sugar and butter and beat until creamy.
3. Add the eggs and whisk until blended nicely.
4. In another bowl, sift together the flour, salt and baking powder.
5. Add the egg mixture, milk, vanilla and lemon juice and mix until well combined.
6. Gently, fold in the peach pieces.
7. Add desired amount of the mixture in waffle iron and cook as suggested by the manufacturer.
8. Repeat with the remaining mixture.
9. Enjoy warm.

HOW TO
a Waffle

🥣 Prep Time: 5 mins
🕐 Total Time: 10 mins

Servings per Recipe: 4
Calories 581.8
Fat 33.0g
Cholesterol 67.8mg
Sodium 724.8mg
Carbohydrates 60.1g
Protein 11.5g

Ingredients

2 C. flour
4 tsp baking powder
1/2 tsp salt
2 tbsp sugar
1/2 C. vegetable oil

1 3/4 C. milk
1 egg

Directions

1. In a bowl, sift together the flour and baking powder.
2. Add the sugar and salt and mix well.
3. Add the remaining ingredients and mix until well combined.
4. Add desired amount of the mixture in waffle iron and cook for about 5-6 minutes.
5. Repeat with the remaining mixture.
6. Enjoy warm.

Flat Waffle Cookies (Pizelles)

Prep Time: 10 mins
Total Time: 40 mins

Servings per Recipe: 60
Calories   95.2
Fat   3.9g
Cholesterol   21.1mg
Sodium   49.1mg
Carbohydrates   13.2g
Protein   1.5g

Ingredients

- 6 large eggs, beaten
- 2 C. granulated sugar
- 1/2 C. margarine, melted and cooled
- 1/2 C. canola oil
- 1 tsp vanilla
- 1 tsp almond extract
- 3 tbsp anise extract
- 4 C. all-purpose white flour
- 4 tsp baking powder
- powdered sugar

Directions

1. Set your pizelle iron and lightly, grease it.
2. In a bowl, mix together the flour and baking powder.
3. In another bowl, add the sugar and eggs and beat until creamy.
4. Add the margarine and mix well.
5. Slowly, add the flour mixture, 1 C. at a time and mix until just combined.
6. Add desired amount of the mixture in waffle iron and cook as suggested by the manufacturer.
7. Repeat with the remaining mixture.
8. Enjoy warm with a dusting of the powdered sugar.

WAFFLES
French Toast Style II

Prep Time: 10 mins
Total Time: 30 mins

Servings per Recipe: 4
Calories   804.8
Fat   13.2g
Cholesterol   114.6mg
Sodium   1650.9mg
Carbohydrates   139.9g
Protein   28.1g

Ingredients

1 C. skim milk
1 tbsp sugar
1 tbsp butter, melted
1 tsp vanilla
1/2 tsp cinnamon

2 eggs
16 slices day-old French bread
cooking spray

Directions

1. Set your waffle iron and lightly, grease it.
2. In a bowl, add the butter, sugar, eggs, milk, vanilla and cinnamon and beat until well combined.
3. In the bottom of a 13x9-inch baking dish, arrange the bread slices evenly.
4. Top with the milk mixture and gently, coat the bread pieces with mixture.
5. Keep side for about 5 minutes.
6. Arrange 4 bread slices in the waffle iron. and cook for about 4-5 minutes.
7. Repeat with the remaining bread slices.

November
Gingerbread Waffles

🥣 Prep Time: 15 mins
🕐 Total Time: 30 mins

Servings per Recipe: 8
Calories	209.2
Fat	7.2g
Cholesterol	26.4mg
Sodium	208.0mg
Carbohydrates	34.2g
Protein	2.4g

Ingredients

1/4 C. sugar
1/4 C. shortening
1 egg
1/2 C. molasses
1 C. all-purpose flour
3/4 tsp baking soda
1/4 tsp salt
1 tsp ground ginger
1/2 tsp ground cinnamon
1/4 tsp ground cloves
1/2 C. hot water
sweetened whipped cream
ground cinnamon

Directions

1. Set your waffle iron and lightly, grease it.
2. In a bowl, add the flour, baking soda, spices and salt and mix well.
3. In another bowl, add the shortening and sugar and beat until creamy.
4. Add the molasses and beat until blended nicely.
5. Add the flour mixture and beat until well combined.
6. Add the hot water and stir to combine.
7. Add 1 1/4 C. of the mixture in waffle iron and cook as suggested by the manufacturer.
8. Repeat with the remaining mixture.
9. Enjoy warm a topping of the whipped cream and extra cinnamon.

CINNAMON
Ginger Waffles

🥣 Prep Time: 10 mins
🕐 Total Time: 15 mins

Servings per Recipe: 8
Calories   492.6
Fat   15.8g
Cholesterol   128.8mg
Sodium   641.9mg
Carbohydrates   79.3g
Protein   9.7g

Ingredients

3 C. all-purpose flour
4 tsp baking powder
2 tsp ground cinnamon
1 1/2 tsp ginger, grated
1 tsp salt
4 eggs
2/3 C. brown sugar, packed

2 medium bananas, extra-ripe
1 1/4 C. milk
1/2 C. molasses
1/2 C. butter, melted
powdered sugar

Directions

1. Set your waffle iron and lightly, grease it.
2. In a food processor, add the bananas and pulse until pureed.
3. In a bowl, add the flour, spices, baking powder and salt.
4. In another bowl, add the brown sugar and eggs and beat until creamy.
5. Add the corn syrup, molasses, milk and pureed bananas and beat until well combined.
6. Add the flour mixture and mix until just combined.
7. Add 3/4 C. of the mixture in waffle iron and cook as suggested by the manufacturer.
8. Repeat with the remaining mixture.
9. Enjoy warm with a sprinkling of the powdered sugar.

Skytop Waffles

Prep Time: 5 mins
Total Time: 8 mins

Servings per Recipe: 1
Calories	3840.5
Fat	226.5g
Cholesterol	1633.4mg
Sodium	8508.2mg
Carbohydrates	362.4g
Protein	106.0g

Ingredients

- 1 1/2 C. buckwheat flour
- 1 1/2 C. flour
- 4 tsp baking powder
- 1 1/2 tsp baking soda
- 1 tsp salt
- 4 tbsp sugar
- 6 eggs
- 3 C. buttermilk
- 1 C. melted and cooled butter

Directions

1. Set your waffle iron and lightly, grease it.
2. In a bowl, add the flours, baking soda, baking powder, sugar and salt and mix well.
3. In another bowl, add the butter, eggs and buttermilk and beat until blended nicely.
4. Add the flour mixture and mix until just combined.
5. Add desired amount of the mixture in waffle iron and cook as suggested by the manufacturer.
6. Repeat with the remaining mixture.
7. Enjoy warm.

PB&J Waffles

Prep Time: 10 mins
Total Time: 20 mins

Servings per Recipe: 10
Calories   187.2
Fat   10.0g
Cholesterol   50.6mg
Sodium   239.7mg
Carbohydrates   19.2g
Protein   6.0g

Ingredients

1 1/4 C. all-purpose flour
3 tbsp sugar
1 tbsp baking powder
1/4 tsp baking soda
1/4 tsp ground cinnamon
2 eggs, separated
1 1/4 C. milk

1/3 C. peanut butter
3 tbsp butter, melted
jelly

Directions

1. In a bowl, add the flour, sugar, baking soda, baking powder and cinnamon and mix well.
2. In another bowl, add the butter, peanut butter, milk and egg yolks and beat until well combined.
3. Add the flour mixture and mix until just combined.
4. In a glass bowl, add the egg whites and beat until stiff peaks form.
5. Gently, fold the whipped egg whites into the flour mixture.
6. Add the flour mixture and mix until just combined.
7. Add desired amount of the mixture in waffle iron and cook as suggested by the manufacturer.
8. Repeat with the remaining mixture.
9. Enjoy warm with a topping of the jelly.

Maryland Chicken Waffles

Prep Time: 12 hrs
Total Time: 12 hrs 20 mins

Servings per Recipe: 2
Calories   904.6
Fat   59.4g
Cholesterol   95.8mg
Sodium   1057.3mg
Carbohydrates   53.4g
Protein   37.6g

Ingredients

8 oz. chicken breasts, chucks
1/4 C. buttermilk
1/2 tsp seasoning salt
1/4 tsp ground black pepper
1/4 tsp paprika
1/4 C. canola oil
1 C. panko breadcrumbs

8 slices turkey bacon
2 Pillsbury grands refrigerated biscuits
maple syrup

Directions

1. In a bowl, add the buttermilk, chicken pieces, seasoned salt, paprika and black pepper and mix well.
2. Refrigerate to marinate for whole night.
3. Remove the chicken pieces from the marinade and coat with the breadcrumbs evenly.
4. Place a large skillet over high heat until heated through.
5. Add the bacon and cook for about 8-10 minutes.
6. With a slotted spoon, place the bacon onto a paper towel-lined plate to drain.
7. In the same skillet, add the oil with the bacon grease over high heat and cook the chicken pieces for about 3-4 minutes per side.
8. With a slotted spoon, place the chicken into a bowl.
9. Now, crumble the bacon into small pieces and divide into 3 equal sized parts.
10. Open the Pillsbury Biscuits dough packages.
11. Place 1 part of the bacon bits over one dough and with your palms, pat into a 7-inch circle.
12. Repeat with the second dough.
13. Set your waffle iron and lightly, grease it.

14. Arrange 1 dough circle into the waffle iron and cook for about 5 minutes.
15. Repeat with the second dough circle.
16. Arrange the waffles onto serving plates and drizzle with the maple syrup.
17. Divide chicken and remaining bacon part over each waffle and enjoy.

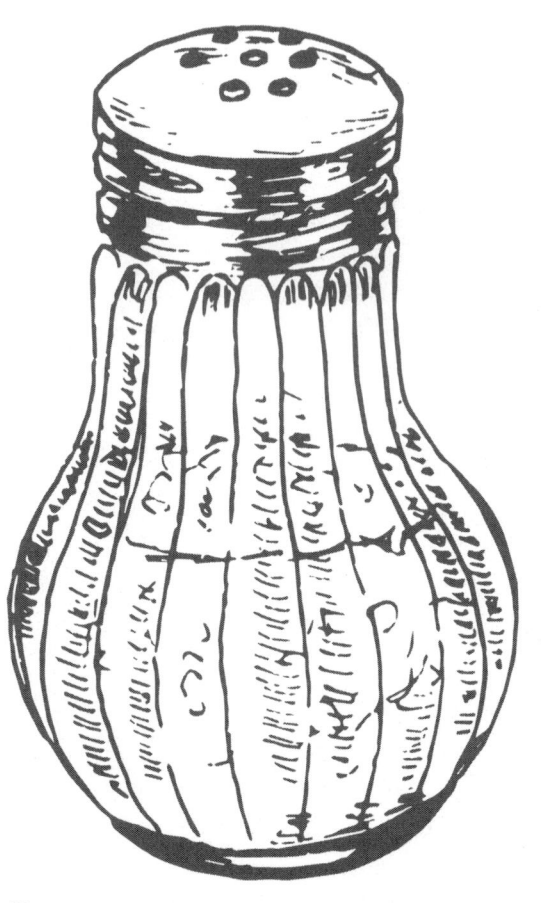

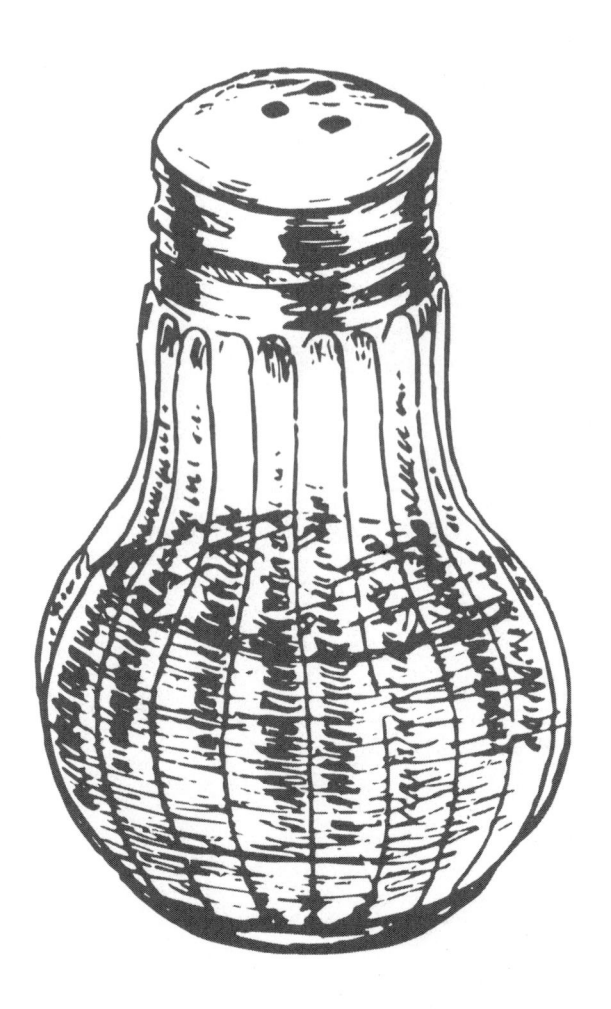

Cake Flour Waffles

Prep Time: 10 mins
Total Time: 15 mins

Servings per Recipe: 1
Calories 271.5
Fat 17.2g
Cholesterol 97.6mg
Sodium 467.0mg
Carbohydrates 23.9g
Protein 5.5g

Ingredients

1/2 C. butter, melted
1 tbsp sugar
2 egg yolks
2 egg whites, beaten
1 C. buttermilk
1 pinch salt

1 C. cake flour
1 tbsp cake flour
4 tsp baking powder

Directions

1. Set your waffle iron and lightly, grease it.
2. In a bowl, sift together the flour, baking powder and salt.
3. In a bowl, add the sugar and butter and beat until creamy.
4. Add the egg yolks and mix well.
5. Add the flour mixture and milk and mix until just combined.
6. In a glass bowl, add the egg whites and beat until stiff peaks form.
7. Gently, fold the whipped egg whites into the flour mixture.
8. Add desired amount of the mixture in waffle iron and cook as suggested by the manufacturer.
9. Repeat with the remaining mixture.
10. Enjoy warm.

SIMPLE
Vanilla Waffles

Prep Time: 25 mins
Total Time: 25 mins

Servings per Recipe: 6
Calories 517.2
Fat 27.2g
Cholesterol 189.6mg
Sodium 981.3mg
Carbohydrates 54.0g
Protein 13.5g

Ingredients

3 C. sifted flour
4 tsp double-acting baking powder
1 tsp salt
2 tsp sugar
2/3 C. butter, melted

2 C. milk
4 eggs, separated
1 tsp vanilla

Directions

1. In a bowl, add the flour, sugar, baking powder and salt and mix well.
2. In another bowl, add the milk, egg yolks and vanilla and beat until well combined.
3. Add the flour mixture and mix until just combined.
4. Add the butter and mix until well combined.
5. In a glass bowl, add the egg whites and beat until stiff peaks form.
6. Gently, fold the whipped egg whites into the flour mixture.
7. Add 14 oz. of the mixture in waffle iron and cook as suggested by the manufacturer.
8. Repeat with the remaining mixture.
9. Enjoy warm.

Georgia Peach and Biscuit Waffles

Prep Time: 15 mins
Total Time: 40 mins

Servings per Recipe: 4
Calories   845.3
Fat   41.4g
Cholesterol   63.1mg
Sodium   1641.4mg
Carbohydrates   107.1g
Protein   13.9g

Ingredients

- 3 oz. cream cheese
- 1/4 C. ricotta cheese
- 2 tbsp powdered sugar
- 1 tsp vanilla extract
- 1/4 tsp lemon juice
- 1/4 tsp lemon zest
- 2 large ripe peaches, halved and pitted
- 2 (10 count) cans refrigerated biscuits
- 4 tbsp melted butter
- 1 tbsp honey
- 1/2 C. granulated sugar
- 2 tsp cinnamon
- 2 pieces Reynolds Wrap Foil

Directions

1. Set your oven to 375 degrees F before doing anything else and arrange 2 foil pieces onto a baking sheet.
2. In a bowl, add the ricotta cheese, cream cheese and powdered sugar and beat until smooth.
3. Add the lemon zest, lemon juice and vanilla and stir until blended nicely.
4. Place in the fridge until using.
5. In a bowl, add 1 tbsp of the honey and 1 tbsp of the butter and mix well.
6. Arrange 2 peach halves onto 1 foil pieces, skin side down.
7. Coat each peach half with the honey mixture evenly.
8. Fold each foil over the peach halves to create a pouch.
9. Cook in the oven for about 15-20 minutes.
10. Set your waffle iron and lightly, grease it.
11. In a shallow plate, place the remaining 3 tbsp of the butter.
12. In another shallow plate, add the granulated sugar and cinnamon and mix well.
13. With the palms of your hands, pat each biscuit and shape into a small disk.

14. Coat each disk with the melted butter and then with the cinnamon sugar.
15. Arrange the coated disks into waffle iron in batches and cook for about 3 minutes.
16. Transfer the cooked waffles onto a platter and with a piece of foil, cover them to keep warm.
17. Remove the peaches from the oven.
18. Careful, open the foil pouches to cool the peaches.
19. Arrange 5 waffles onto each serving plate.
20. Place about 1 tbsp of the cream cheese mixture in the center of each peach half.
21. Carefully, place 1 peach half over the waffles in each plate.
22. Enjoy warm with a drizzling of the remaining honey butter.

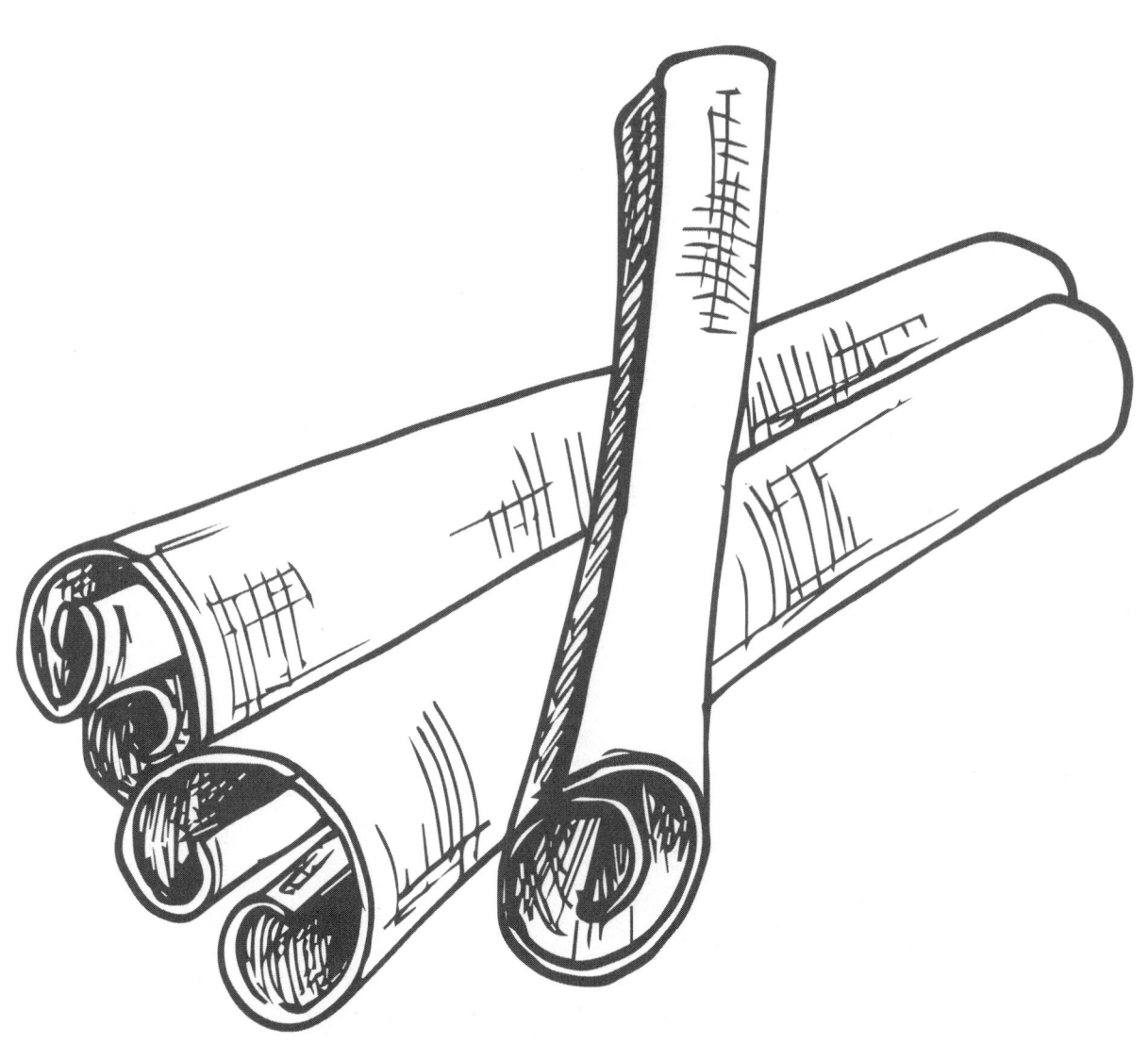

Dijon Buttermilk Waffles

Prep Time: 30 mins
Total Time: 30 mins

Servings per Recipe: 4
Calories   335.5
Fat   16.3g
Cholesterol   145.7mg
Sodium   740.3mg
Carbohydrates   33.0g
Protein   14.3g

Ingredients

- 2/3 C. flour
- 2/3 C. rye flour
- 1/4 tsp baking soda
- 1 tsp baking powder
- 1/2 tsp salt
- 2 eggs, beaten
- 1 C. buttermilk
- 2 tbsp melted butter
- 2 tbsp chopped scallions
- 1/2 tsp Dijon mustard
- 3/4 C. grated smoked cheddar cheese

Directions

1. In a bowl, add the flours, baking powder, baking soda and salt.
2. In another bowl, add the cheese, butter, buttermilk, eggs, mustard and scallions and beat until well combined.
3. Add the flour mixture and mix until just blended.
4. Keep the mixture aside for about 9-10 minutes.
5. Set your waffle iron and lightly, grease it.
6. Add 1/3 C. of the mixture in waffle iron and cook as suggested by the manufacturer.
7. Repeat with the remaining mixture.
8. Enjoy warm.

WAFFLE
Sandwiches

🥣 Prep Time: 15 mins
🕐 Total Time: 30 mins

Servings per Recipe: 4
Calories   780.5
Fat   32.2g
Cholesterol   57.4mg
Sodium   629.0mg
Carbohydrates   117.7g
Protein   9.4g

Ingredients

8 frozen waffles
2 (3 oz.) packages cream cheese, softened
1/2 C. packed brown sugar
1/2 tsp ground cinnamon
1 tsp vanilla extract
1/2 C. chopped pecans

1 C. maple syrup
confectioners' sugar
4 strawberries, halved

Directions

1. In a bowl, add the cream cheese, vanilla, brown sugar and cinnamon and beat until smooth.
2. Add the pecans and stir to combine.
3. Toast the waffles as suggested on the package.
4. Arrange 4 waffles onto serving plates.
5. Place cream cheese mixture over these waffles evenly and cover with the remaining waffles.
6. Drizzle each waffle sandwich with the maple syrup and dust with the confectioners' sugar.
7. Enjoy with a garnishing of the fruit.

Country Crispy Waffles

Prep Time: 11 mins
Total Time: 15 mins

Servings per Recipe: 1
Calories	310.4
Fat	16.6g
Cholesterol	52.9mg
Sodium	383.8mg
Carbohydrates	34.5g
Protein	5.1g

Ingredients

- 1 1/4 C. all-purpose flour
- 1 C. rice krispies cereal
- 3/4 C. cornstarch
- 1/4 C. sugar
- 1 tsp baking powder
- 1/2 tsp baking soda
- 3/4 tsp table salt
- 2 large eggs, separated
- 1 1/2 C. milk
- 1 tsp vanilla extract
- 1/2 C. vegetable oil

Directions

1. Set your waffle iron to medium setting and lightly, grease it.
2. In a bowl, add the cornstarch, Rice Krispies, flour, sugar, baking soda, baking powder and salt and mix well.
3. In another bowl, add the oil, milk, egg yolks and vanilla and beat until well combined.
4. add the flour mixture and mix until just combined.
5. In a glass bowl, add the egg whites and beat until soft peaks form.
6. Gently, fold the whipped egg whites into the flour mixture.
7. Add 2/3 C. of the mixture in waffle iron and cook for about 3-4 minutes.
8. Repeat with the remaining mixture.
9. Enjoy warm.

GREEN FETA
Waffles

🍲 Prep Time: 15 mins
🕒 Total Time: 15 mins

Servings per Recipe: 1
Calories	633.4
Fat	38.6g
Cholesterol	128.0mg
Sodium	691.8mg
Carbohydrates	55.0g
Protein	16.3g

Ingredients

1 egg, separated
1 C. all-purpose flour
1 tsp baking powder
1/8 tsp salt
1/2-1 tsp sugar
1/8 tsp garlic powder
1/4 tsp dried dill

3/4 C. milk
1/3 C. crumbled feta cheese
1/3 C. cooked spinach, well drained and chopped
4 tbsp olive oil

Directions

1. Set your waffle iron and lightly, grease it.
2. In a bowl, add the flour, sugar, baking powder, dried dill, garlic powder and salt and mix well.
3. In another bowl, add the oil, milk, egg yolk and feta cheese and mix until well combined.
4. Add the flour mixture and mix until just combined.
5. In a glass bowl, add the egg whites and beat until stiff peaks form.
6. Gently, fold the whipped egg whites into the flour mixture.
7. Add the flour mixture and mix until just combined.
8. Add desired amount of the mixture in waffle iron and cook as suggested by the manufacturer.
9. Repeat with the remaining mixture.
10. Enjoy warm.

Leftover Rice Waffles with Spiced Syrup

Prep Time: 15 mins
Total Time: 23 mins

Servings per Recipe: 1
Calories   304.5
Fat   8.1g
Cholesterol   66.7mg
Sodium   383.2mg
Carbohydrates   54.8g
Protein   4.8g

Ingredients

1 C. sifted flour
2 tsp baking powder
2 tbsp sugar
3/4 tsp salt
2 egg yolks, beaten
1 C. milk
2 tbsp melted butter
1 C. cooked rice
2 egg whites, beaten

Flavored Syrup
1/2 C. honey
1/2 C. maple syrup
1/2 tsp caraway seed
1 tsp ground cinnamon
2 tbsp butter

Directions

1. Set your waffle iron and lightly, grease it.
2. In a bowl, add the flour, sugar, baking powder and salt and mix well. Now, sift the flour mixture into another bowl.
3. In another bowl, add the butter, milk and egg yolks and beat until well combined.
4. Add the flour mixture and mix until just combined.
5. In a glass bowl, add the egg whites and beat until stiff peaks form.
6. Gently, fold the cooked rice and whipped egg whites into the flour mixture. Add desired amount of the mixture in waffle iron and cook as suggested by the manufacturer.
7. Repeat with the remaining mixture.
8. Meanwhile, for syrup: in a pan, add the butter, maple syrup, honey, caraway seeds and cinnamon and cook until boiling, stirring continuously. Enjoy the waffles warm with a topping of the syrup.

LUNCH
Pizza Waffles

Prep Time: 5 mins
Total Time: 10 mins

Servings per Recipe: 1
Calories   65.1
Fat   3.8g
Cholesterol   11.0mg
Sodium   238.0mg
Carbohydrates   3.8g
Protein   3.7g

Ingredients

1 frozen gluten-free waffle, toasted
2 -3 tbsp pizza sauce
6 pepperoni slices

2 tbsp mozzarella cheese

Directions

1. Set your oven to broiler.
2. Place the pizza sauce over waffle evenly and top with the pepperoni, followed by the mozzarella cheese.
3. Cook under the broiler until the cheese is melted.
4. Enjoy warm.

4-Ingredient American Breakfast (Quick Waffle Sandwich)

Prep Time: 10 mins
Total Time: 20 mins

Servings per Recipe: 2
Calories   872.8
Fat   58.7g
Cholesterol   380.7mg
Sodium   1869.5mg
Carbohydrates   52.4g
Protein   31.7g

Ingredients

4 toaster waffles, toasted
1/2 lb. sausage, made into 2 patties
2 large eggs, beaten

softened butter

Directions

1. Heat a frying pan and cook the sausage patties until cooked through.
2. In another lightly, greased frying pan, cook the eggs until scrambled.
3. Spread the butter on one side of each waffle.
4. Arrange 2 waffles onto serving plate, butter side up and top each with the scrambled egg and sausage patty evenly.
5. Cover with the remaining waffles, buttered side down.

SWEET Mediterranean Waffles

Prep Time: 10 mins
Total Time: 30 mins

Servings per Recipe: 8
Calories 140.4
Fat 3.7g
Cholesterol 69.7mg
Sodium 308.8mg
Carbohydrates 21.6g
Protein 4.8g

Ingredients

1 1/2 C. all-purpose flour
1/2 tsp salt
1 tbsp baking powder
1 tbsp sugar
3 eggs
1 1/2 C. non-fat vanilla yogurt
2 tbsp cinnamon
1 tsp vanilla
1 tbsp oil

Directions

1. Set your waffle iron and lightly, grease it.
2. In a bowl, add the flour and baking powder and mix well.
3. In another bowl, add the yogurt, sugar, eggs, vanilla and salt and beat until well combined.
4. Add the flour mixture and mix until just combined.
5. Add desired amount of the mixture in waffle iron and cook as suggested by the manufacturer.
6. Repeat with the remaining mixture.
7. Enjoy warm.

Cornmeal Cereal Waffles

🥣 Prep Time: 10 mins
🕐 Total Time: 20 mins

Servings per Recipe: 1
Calories   355.7
Fat   7.0g
Cholesterol   60.9mg
Sodium   307.8mg
Carbohydrates   67.0g
Protein   7.2g

Ingredients

Waffle
3 C. Fruit Loops cereal
1 3/4 C. all-purpose flour
2 tbsp cornmeal
1 tbsp sugar
1 tbsp baking powder
1/4 tsp salt
2 eggs

2 C. whole milk
2 tbsp unsalted butter, cooled
Glaze
4 tbsp whole milk
2 C. powdered sugar

Directions

1. Set your waffle iron and lightly, grease it.
2. In a blender, add the cereal and pulse until a coarse crumb like mixture is formed.
3. In a bowl, add the cornmeal, flour, sugar, baking powder and salt and mix well.
4. In another bowl, add the milk, butter and eggs and until well combined.
5. Add the flour mixture and stir until just blended.
6. Gently, fold in the cereal crumbs.
7. Add desired amount of the mixture in waffle iron and cook as suggested by the manufacturer.
8. Repeat with the remaining mixture.
9. Meanwhile, for the glaze: in a bowl, add the powdered sugar and milk and beat until smooth.
10. Divide the waffles onto serving plates and top with the glaze.
11. Enjoy warm with a garnishing of the extra cereal.

HONEY
Hazel Waffles

🥣 Prep Time: 30 mins
🕐 Total Time: 1 hr

Servings per Recipe: 5
Calories   833.7
Fat   45.2g
Cholesterol   203.2mg
Sodium   613.9mg
Carbohydrates   89.9g
Protein   19.5g

Ingredients

1/2 C. unsalted butter
1/4 C. honey
3 1/2 C. all-purpose flour
1 tbsp baking powder
1/2 tsp salt
1/4 tsp baking soda
3 large eggs
1 1/2 C. whole milk

1 C. sour cream
2/3 C. chopped toasted hazelnuts
Pam cooking spray
confectioners' sugar
maple syrup

Directions

1. Set your waffle iron and lightly, grease it.
2. In a pan, add the honey and butter over low heat and cook until melted, stirring frequently.
3. Remove from the heat and keep aside.
4. In a bowl, add the flour, baking soda, baking powder and salt and mix well.
5. In another bowl, add the sour cream, milk and eggs and beat until well combined.
6. Slowly, add the flour mixture and mix until well combined.
7. Add the honey mixture and hazelnuts and gently stir to combine.
8. Add 1 C. of the mixture in waffle iron and cook as suggested by the manufacturer.
9. Repeat with the remaining mixture.
10. Enjoy warm.

Vegetarian Soy Waffles

Prep Time: 5 mins
Total Time: 15 mins

Servings per Recipe: 4
Calories	234.0
Fat	13.3g
Cholesterol	0.0mg
Sodium	491.8mg
Carbohydrates	23.9g
Protein	4.8g

Ingredients

3/4 C. flour
2 tsp baking powder
1/4 tsp salt
1 tsp sugar
1 tbsp ground flax seeds
1/4 C. melted margarine
1 C. soymilk

Directions

1. In a bowl, add the flour, sugar, baking powder and salt and mix well.
2. In another bowl, add the milk, margarine and flax seeds and mix well.
3. Gently, fold the flax seeds mixture into the flour mixture.
4. Add 1/3 C. of the mixture in waffle iron and cook as suggested by the manufacturer.
5. Repeat with the remaining mixture.
6. Enjoy warm.

RACHELA'S
Red Velvet Waffles

Prep Time: 30 mins
Total Time: 40 mins

Servings per Recipe: 4
Calories 662.9
Fat 15.8g
Cholesterol 128.4mg
Sodium 727.7mg
Carbohydrates 117.4g
Protein 14.1g

Ingredients

2 C. flour
1 1/4 C. sugar
1/4 tsp salt
1 tsp baking soda
4 tsp unsweetened cocoa powder
1/4 C. butter, melted, cooled
2 C. buttermilk
2 large eggs, separated

1 tsp vanilla
2 tbsp red food coloring

Directions

1. Set your waffle iron and lightly, grease it.
2. In a bowl, add the flour, sugar, cocoa powder, baking soda and salt and mix well.
3. Add the butter, buttermilk, egg yolks, vanilla and food coloring and mix until well combined.
4. In a glass bowl, add the egg whites and beat until stiff peaks form.
5. Gently, fold the whipped egg whites into the flour mixture.
6. Add desired amount of the mixture in waffle iron and cook as suggested by the manufacturer.
7. Repeat with the remaining mixture.
8. Enjoy warm.

Canadian Chocolate Waffles

🥣 Prep Time: 15 mins
🕐 Total Time: 25 mins

Servings per Recipe: 1
Calories   357.9
Fat   22.0g
Cholesterol   31.4mg
Sodium   385.1mg
Carbohydrates   38.6g
Protein   7.4g

Ingredients

- 100 g desiccated coconut
- 1/2 tsp salt
- 2 tsp maple syrup
- 1 tbsp coconut oil
- 190 g flour, gluten free
- 25 g unsweetened cocoa powder
- 1 egg
- 15 ml maple syrup
- 1/2 tsp baking soda
- 5 g baking powder
- 250 ml milk
- 60 ml olive oil
- 1/2 tsp vanilla extract
- 80 g bittersweet chocolate chips
- 1 nonstick cooking spray

Directions

1. Set your waffle iron and lightly, grease it.
2. for the coconut butter: in a blender, add the coconut, 2 tsp of the maple syrup, coconut oil and salt and pulse until well combined.
3. In a bowl, add the flour, cocoa powder, baking soda, baking powder and remaining maple syrup and mix until well combined.
4. With a spoon, create a well in the middle of the flour mixture.
5. In the well of the flour mixture, add the oil, milk, egg yolk and vanilla and mix until just blended
6. In a glass bowl, add the egg whites and beat until soft peaks form.
7. Gently, fold the whipped egg whites into the flour mixture.
8. Gently, fold in the chocolate chips.
9. Add desired amount of the mixture in waffle iron and cook for about 3 minutes.
10. Repeat with the remaining mixture.
11. Enjoy warm with a topping of the coconut butter.

CUTE Waffles

Prep Time: 30 mins
Total Time: 35 mins

Servings per Recipe: 8
Calories 430.2
Fat 19.6g
Cholesterol 181.9mg
Sodium 849.9mg
Carbohydrates 50.5g
Protein 12.3g

Ingredients

6 eggs, separated
1 C. milk
4 C. all-purpose flour
8 tsp baking powder
1 tsp salt

10 tbsp butter, melted
gel food coloring

Directions

1. In a bowl, add the flour, baking powder and salt and mix well.
2. In another bowl, add the milk and egg yolks and beat well.
3. Add the flour mixture and mix until just combined.
4. In a glass bowl, add the egg whites and beat until stiff peaks form.
5. Gently, fold the whipped egg whites into the flour mixture.
6. Now, sift the flour mixture into another bowl.
7. In 6 bowl, divide the mixture evenly.
8. Add enough amount of each color in 1 bowl and stir to combine.
9. In each of 6 Ziploc bag, place 1 colored mixture.
10. Pipe each mixture in circles in waffle iron and cook as suggested by the manufacturer.
11. Enjoy warm.

Vegan Papaya and Orange Waffles

Prep Time: 5 mins
Total Time: 15 mins

Servings per Recipe: 2
Calories	511.7
Fat	23.7g
Cholesterol	0.0mg
Sodium	530.6mg
Carbohydrates	75.8g
Protein	7.4g

Ingredients

- 30 g flour
- 15 g arrowroot
- 15 g coconut flour
- 20 g tiger nuts, or almonds
- 100 g bananas
- 120 g coconut milk
- 20 g water
- 50 g orange juice
- 25 g maple syrup
- 3 g baking soda
- 20 g apple cider vinegar
- 1/2 papaya
- 2 dried figs
- 2 tbsp coconut flakes, shredded
- 10 g dark chocolate, shaved

Directions

1. Set your waffle iron and lightly, grease it.
2. In a bowl, add the flours, arrowroot and tiger nuts and mix until well combined.
3. In a food processor, add the orange juice, coconut milk, water and banana and pulse until well combined.
4. Place the banana mixture and maple syrup in the bowl of the flour mixture and mix until blended nicely.
5. Add in the vinegar and baking soda and mix until blended nicely.
6. Add half of the mixture in waffle iron and cook as suggested by the manufacturer.
7. Repeat with the remaining mixture.
8. Enjoy warm with a topping of the papaya, figs, coconut and chocolate shaving.

SPICY
Cheddar Waffles

🥣 Prep Time: 5 mins
🕐 Total Time: 40 mins

Servings per Recipe: 4
Calories   653.6
Fat   36.8g
Cholesterol   155.3mg
Sodium   1041.1mg
Carbohydrates   56.0g
Protein   25.4g

Ingredients

1 C. all-purpose flour
1 C. cornmeal
1 tbsp sugar
1 tbsp baking powder
1 jalapeño, seeded and diced
1/2 tsp kosher salt
2 C. grated sharp cheddar cheese
2 large eggs

1 1/4 C. buttermilk
1/4 C. vegetable oil
nonstick cooking spray

Directions

1. Set your waffle iron and lightly, grease it.
2. In a bowl, add the cornmeal, flour, sugar, baking powder, salt, 1 C. of the cheese and jalapeño and mix well.
3. In another bowl, add the oil, buttermilk and eggs and beat until well combined.
4. Add the flour mixture and mix until just blended.
5. Add 1 1/2 C. of the mixture in waffle iron and cook as suggested by the manufacturer.
6. Repeat with the remaining mixture.
7. Meanwhile, set the broiler of your oven to low and arrange a rack onto a baking sheet.
8. arrange the waffles onto the prepared baking sheet and sprinkle with the remaining 1 C. of the cheese evenly.
9. Cook under the broiler for about 1 minute.
10. Enjoy warm.

Seattle Waffles with Avocados

Prep Time: 15 mins
Total Time: 35 mins

Servings per Recipe: 4
Calories	724.6
Fat	40.0g
Cholesterol	389.4mg
Sodium	1240.5mg
Carbohydrates	67.9g
Protein	25.5g

Ingredients

Waffles
2 C. all-purpose flour
4 tsp baking powder
1 tbsp granulated sugar
1/2 tsp salt
2 large eggs
1 1/2 C. whole milk
1 C. mashed cooked purple sweet potato
3 tbsp vegetable oil
Garnish
2 medium avocados, peeled, pitted and chopped
1 tbsp lime juices
1/2 tsp salt
1/2 tsp black pepper
1/2 tsp crushed red pepper flakes
6 fried eggs
1/2 a red onion, sliced
1/4 C. crumbled feta cheese
2 tbsp chopped parsley

Directions

1. Set your waffle iron and lightly, grease it.
2. For the waffles, in a large bowl, add the flour, sugar, baking powder and salt and mix well.
3. In another bowl, add the remaining ingredients and beat until blended nicely.
4. Add the flour mixture and mix until just combined.
5. Add 1/3 C. of the mixture in waffle iron and cook as suggested by the manufacturer. Repeat with the remaining mixture.
6. Meanwhile, for the topping: in a bowl, add the avocado, lime juice, a pinch of red pepper flakes, salt and pepper and with a fork, mash well.
7. Divide the waffles onto serving plates and top each with a little mashed avocado, followed by 1 fried egg, onion, feta cheese and parsley.
8. Enjoy with a sprinkling of the red pepper flakes.

FULL GEORGIA
Breakfast (Sausage, Waffles, and Home Fries)

Prep Time: 10 mins
Total Time: 35 mins

Servings per Recipe: 4
Calories	843.3
Fat	44.9 g
Cholesterol	251.8 mg
Sodium	2038.1 mg
Carbohydrates	80.3 g
Protein	31.0 g

Ingredients

Waffles
1/2 C. unsalted butter, melted and cooled
3 large eggs
1 1/2 C. buttermilk
1 tsp vanilla
1 3/4 C. all-purpose flour
2 tsp baking powder
1 tsp baking soda
1/2 tsp salt
1 medium zucchini, shredded
1 (10 oz.) boxes frozen spinach, thawed and well drained
Potatoes
1 (8 oz.) packages beef breakfast sausage
1 C. yellow onion, diced
3 medium Yukon gold potatoes, diced
2 medium carrots, diced
1 small medium bell pepper, diced
1 tsp salt
1/2 tsp black pepper
1/4 C. chopped parsley

Directions

1. For the waffles: in a bowl, add the flour, baking soda, baking powder and salt.
2. In another bowl, add the milk, eggs, butter and vanilla and beat until blended nicely.
3. Add the flour mixture and mix until just moistened.
4. Add the spinach and zucchini and gently, stir to combine.
5. Add 1/3 C. of the mixture in waffle iron and cook as suggested by the manufacturer.
6. Repeat with the remaining mixture.
7. Meanwhile, for the hash, place a wok over medium-high heat until heated through.
8. Add the sausage and cook for about 7 minutes, breaking with a wooden spoon.
9. Add the carrots, potatoes, bell pepper, onion, salt and pepper and stir to combine.
10. Set the heat to medium and cook for about 13-16 minutes, mixing occasionally.
11. Divide the waffles onto serving plates and top each with the sausage hash evenly.
12. Enjoy with a garnishing of the parsley.

Waffles Brulee

Prep Time: 25 mins
Total Time: 55 mins

Servings per Recipe: 1
Calories 733.4
Fat 44.7g
Cholesterol 220.2mg
Sodium 1190.4mg
Carbohydrates 68.1g
Protein 14.8g

Ingredients

Filling
1 lb. cream cheese
1 C. powdered sugar
2 tsp vanilla extract
1 large pinch kosher salt
Waffles
2 C. all-purpose flour
1 tbsp baking soda
1/2 tsp kosher salt
1/4 C. light brown sugar
3 large eggs
2 C. buttermilk
1/2 C. melted unsalted butter
1 tsp vanilla extract
2 1/2 C. turbinado sugar

Directions

1. For the cream cheese filling: in a bowl, add all the ingredients and with a hand mixer, mix until well combined.
2. Set your waffle iron to the medium heat setting and lightly, grease it. For the waffles: in a bowl, add the flour, salt and baking soda and mix well.
3. Add the flour mixture and mix until just combined.
4. In a glass bowl, add the egg whites and beat until medium stiff peaks form. Gently, fold the whipped egg whites into the flour mixture.
5. In the bottom of the heated waffle iron, place about 4 tbsp of the turbinado sugar.
6. Place 1 C. of the waffle mixture over the sugar evenly and top with about 4 tbsp of the filling, followed by 1 tbsp the turbinado sugar.
7. Cook for about 2-3 minutes.
8. With the cooking spray, grease the top of the waffle iron.
9. Place 1 tbsp the turbinado sugar over waffle evenly and cook for about 1 minute further. Repeat with the remaining mixture.
10. Enjoy warm.

SARATOGA
Flax Waffles

🥣 Prep Time: 20 mins
🕐 Total Time: 23 mins

Servings per Recipe: 6
Calories   237.1
Fat   14.1g
Cholesterol   66.0mg
Sodium   612.2mg
Carbohydrates   20.1g
Protein   6.3g

Ingredients

1 C. teff flour
1 C. all-purpose flour
1/4 C. flax seed meal
sugar
1 tbsp baking powder
1 tsp sea salt
1/4 C. vegetable oil
2 eggs

1 tbsp vanilla
1 C. whole milk
fruit

Directions

1. In a bowl, add the flour, flax seed meal, sugar, baking powder and salt and mix well.
2. Add half C. of the milk, oil, eggs and vanilla and mix well.
3. Add the fruit and stir to combine.
4. Add the remaining milk and mix until smooth.
5. Add desired amount of the mixture in waffle iron and cook as suggested by the manufacturer.
6. Repeat with the remaining mixture.
7. Enjoy warm.

Yuan's Chinese Egg Waffles

Prep Time: 5 mins
Total Time: 10 mins

Servings per Recipe: 1
Calories   358.1
Fat   18.3g
Cholesterol   187.1mg
Sodium   410.6mg
Carbohydrates   38.2g
Protein   8.3g

Ingredients

4 eggs, separated
1/4 C. milk
1 tbsp vanilla extract
6 tbsp butter, melted
1/4 C. sugar
1 1/4 C. cake flour
1 1/2 tsp baking powder
1 pinch nutmeg, grated
1/4 tsp salt

canola oil
Garnish
powdered sugar
syrup
fruit
coconut

Directions

1. Set your waffle iron and lightly, grease it.
2. In a bowl, add the flour, nutmeg, baking powder and salt and mix well.
3. In another bowl, add the sugar, milk, butter, egg yolks and vanilla and beat until blended nicely.
4. Add the flour mixture and mix until just combined.
5. In a glass bowl, add the egg whites and beat until stiff peaks form.
6. In 3 additions, gently fold the whipped egg whites into the flour mixture.
7. Add desired amount of the mixture in waffle iron and cook for about 2 minutes per side.
8. Repeat with the remaining mixture.
9. Enjoy warm.

ENJOY THE RECIPES?

KEEP ON COOKING WITH 6 MORE FREE COOKBOOKS!

Visit our website and simply enter your email address to join the club and receive your 6 cookbooks.

http://booksumo.com/magnet

https://www.instagram.com/booksumopress/

https://www.facebook.com/booksumo/

Printed in Great Britain
by Amazon